Abercrombie - Porter Debate

Between

Cecil E. Abercrombie
Birmingham, Alabama

and

W. Curtis Porter
Monette, Arkansas

East Point, Georgia
December 4-7, 1951

ISBN 1-58427-062-4

Guardian of Truth Foundation
P.O. Box 9670
Bowling Green, Kentucky 42102

Cecil E. Abercrombie

"DEDICATION"

This debate is printed to fulfill a promise I made to my husband shortly before his death on July 22, 1976.

The discussion occurred some twenty five years earlier, and both parties agreed, at that time, for Bro. Abercrombie to publish this work. Many things hindered in the years that followed, but with great effort and help of good brethren we are now able to do so.

We hope that much good will come from the reading of this book, and that all will be brought closer to the Lord.

Mrs. Cecil (Dorothy) Abercrombie

TABLE OF CONTENTS

INTRODUCTION

Dear Brethren and Friends:

Just a few months before the death of our beloved Cecil Abercrombie, he talked with me quite a lot about his desire to have this debate published. He had great hope and sincerely believed that it would be very helpful and profitable to everyone who has a love for the truth. He especially thought it would be useful for all his brethren.

Here, let me say that after a very careful and prayerful study of the debate, I am thoroughly convinced that I have never seen the truth presented more explicitly, nor error defeated mor successfully than Brother Cecil has done in this discussion. With a candid reading and a love for God's truth, we have no doubt, that you too, will agree.

Here, let me explain or tell you how and why I became involved in writing this preface. Brother Cecil, perhaps knowing that his death was imminent, told me that he would like for me to write something relative to the debate, and say whatever I thought that would be appropriate and informative. I told him that I would. I am also happy to say that his dear wife, Dorothy, concurs with his request. I will forever be thankful and grateful for the confidence that both have entrusted me with in this endeavor. I shall now try to the best of my ability to honor these requests.

To begin with, I want to reiterate some statements that I made while conducting the funeral of Brother Abercrombie. I said that I personally believed that Brother Cecil Abercrombie was one of the great, if not the greatest preachers of our generation. I also stated that to my knowledge, he had few equals, if any, and no superiors, when it comes to preaching the truth, the whole truth and nothing but the truth of our Lord.

Please do not misunderstand me. I am fully aware that there are many great preachers. They have great knowledge, along with ability. We are also thankful to God for every one of them and pray to God to give us many more. But, I hasten to say again, I have yet to meet and hear a preacher that surpassed or was superior to Brother Abercrombie in our generation.

I wish that I could share with you the many things he has done for the cause of Christ, but this would make a large book. We only have space enough to give you some idea of his life and labor for the Lord. He began preaching the glorious gospel of Christ at the age of seventeen. For over thirty-nine years he stood firm, never wavering, always contending earnestly for the faith. He made no effort at elegance of style. Like Paul, his preaching and teaching was not with eticing words of man's wisdom. But, with a thus sayeth the Lord for all that he taught and practiced. When he spoke, he spoke with authority because he spoke as the oracles of God. In all of his preaching he glorified God and exalted Christ, as King and Master, Lord and Saviour. He worked as an evangelist in many states. He has been instrumental in establishing new congregations. He has written many helpful articles and booklets. He has had a number of debates in defense of the gospel.

As to his personal life, those who knew him best will not hesitate to tell you that he was a Christian in every sense of the word. His reputation was flawless. He was not only intensely loyal to the Lord, but also to his friends. He was kind and gentle, charitable and hospitable. His home was your home. He truly was a man of God. I can truly say that everytime I think of him, I thank God for him. Just one other thing I want to tell you about Brother Cecil Abercrombie. Knowing that his death was imminent, he told his loving wife that if there was enough money left over from his insurance, he would like for her to have this debate published. Dear reader, let me ask you to pause here and seriously consider the far-reaching responsibility involved in this request. Knowing that he would soon be with the Lord, he wanted this debate published. I think this is the most unique and profound statement that I have ever heard of, or read about.

Dear friend, what does this tell you? With a just consideration, the answer is obvious. He sincerely believed everything he said in this debate to be the truth. There is no doubt in my mind that Brother Abercrombie has clearly presented the truth and has thoroughly exposed the erroneous and unscriptural Sunday School system of the teaching of his opponent. I assure you kind reader, that what I have said is not a mere lip-service, but what I believe with all my heart. I highly recommend that you prayerfully study what both of our brethren have said, and try them by the word of God. I look forward to its publication. We hope and pray that it will have wide circulation. May God help us all to believe and obey his truth and reject all doctrine and commandments of men.

I think it proper and fitting now, to express our admiration, gratification and appreciation to Sister Dorothy Abercrombie. She has faithfully and loyally proved her devotion to both God and her husband.

I am indeed glad that this debate is being published. We believe that it will accomplish much good in counteracting error and spreading the truth. We brethren in particular, and the public in general, owe a great debt of gratitude to both Brother and Sister Abercrombie, who have made this publication possible. May God bless all who read it to see the truth and obey it.

— Waymon D. Masters —

OPEN DEBATE

Abercrombie-Porter Debate — Beginning Dec. 4, 1951

Proposition:　　The Scriptures Teach That When People Come Together to be Taught by the Church They Should Remain in one Group, and the Teaching Should be done by Men only, One Speaking at a time to the Assembly.

Affirmative:　Cecil Abercrombie Negative: Curtis W. Porter

First Affirmative Speech: Cecil Abercrombie

Brother Porter, Fellow Moderators:

It is a sincere pleasure to stand before this splendid audience tonight in affirmation of that which I sincerely believe to be taught in the precious word of God. I shall, with all the power that God shall give me, present in as lucid a manner that which I believe the Bible to teach, and I shall endeavor to prove my practice concerning the things signed in this proposition by the word of God.

The proposition which has been read before you I wish to read again, and to give a few definitions or explanations. The proposition seems clear enough, but there might be some misunderstanding. "The scriptures teach (I mean the New Testament of Jesus Christ) teaches by command and example the order which I shall set forth, and as defined in this proposition, concerning one group as opposed to the grading, segregating, or dividing the assembly taught by the Church into classes. By the phrase "men only" as opposed to women teaching in church assemblies, speaking one at a time, we mean Just that, or of course, one after the other.

This, my friends, is a serious question. We are divided, We could have greater strength if we marched together united upon what the Bible says. There is no real strength in number when the number is not united upon the truth of the word of God. But we need unity upon a "Thus saith the Lord", upon that which we can plainly read in the scriptures. Jesus Christ prayed that we should all be one. (John 17:20-21)

I shall prove that my teaching and practice is in harmony with God's word as defined in this proposition. My practice, I affirm, is taught in the scriptures. Our practice in this regard has not divided the church of Christ, but the introduction, bringing into the body of Christ, classifying, grouping, and grading, with women teachers has divided the body of Christ, I do not believe the scriptures teach any such thing, Those who contend for that which is not authorized by the Lord are guilty of the sin of division. Just who has the scripture for their practice I trust shall be made known in this discussion. We can all unite on the teaching of the New Testament if we are willing to let the word of God direct us, and I trust that your interest, your presence here tonight is an indication of your interest to know what the Bible teaches, and so therefore without further preliminaries we shall at once go into a consideration of what the Bible teaches.

I now at this time call your attention to the outline. "Teaching When the Church Assembles", God's way or method, or order in teaching when the Church assembles. In 1 Cor. 14:40 the apostle Paul says: "Let all things be done decently and in order". The God of Heaven has given us this divine order. There may be other things that God has not been specific about. We know that concerning the teaching of His word God has given restrictions and regulations, and has restricted the teaching of his precious word; and that is my affirmative tonight — to prove and show to you what God regulates and restricts the teaching of his word as defined in my proposition tonight. We turn to Matthew 28:19. Jesus Christ said, Go ye therefore and make disciples of all the nations, baptizing them into the name of the Father, and of the Son, and of the Holy Spirit", (Revised American Standard Version). King James says, "Go ye therefore and teach all nations." We believe in teaching the precious word of God just as the Bible directs, and strive to do that to the limit of our ability. We find that the Lord said, "Go teach all nations". There is no limit or regulation as to how we go, but the word "teach", we find, is restricted over in the precious word of God, and I shall show those regulations and restrictions to night. It is not as generic as "go", having restrictions in other places of God's word, whereas "go" has no restrictions in any place of the word of God. "Let all things be done decently and in order"; God's order. He gave the order. He did not leave that to man to invent an order that would appear or seem unto him as decent and tho order of things. In this regard God has set forth the order. I am affirming that the church should assemble to be taught the word of God and should not dissemble into various groups with a plurality of teachers teaching at the same time, and men and women all speaking and teaching in a plurality of classes simultaneously. I deny that the word of God teaches such. The word of God does not teach that. In Matthew 18:20, we have authority for assembling, the church to assemble. "Where two or three are gathered together in my name, there am I in their midst." Jesus Christ shows that two or three can assemble to worship God in spirit and in truth and teach His word. We see that a church that small certainly could not have a plurality of classes and teachers all teaching at the same time. The Lord did not institute classifying, grouping and grading and segregating the church into classes with women teaching in those church assemblies.

In Heb. 10:25, the apostle says, "Not forsaking the assembling of yourselves together". So we see that we must come together. In James 2:2, there is a scripture that shows that they had general church assemblies. They came together. There is no indication in the word of the Lord Jesus Christ, in the New Covenant, where the church over came together and then broke into various segments or classified according to human wisdom or any other, to divide up for the purpose of teaching. It is not contained in the word of the Living God. "If there come unto your assembly". Now then, we turn as we shall prove by example, and by commandment that those things are true and that my proposition is true — approved examples, examples in harmony with the word of God and the commands of the Lord.

Now then, we turn to Matthew 16:18 — Jesus Christ said, "Upon this rock I will build My church". The church is the divine teaching institution wherein we find salvation, and that is what we have under consideration tonight, nothing else. We are divided over what the church does when it assembles, and over nothing else as far as the propositions are concerned in this discussion. Jesus Christ said, "I will build My church". We are concerned now about the church when it assembles and how it should teach the word of God. In Acts 2:42, it ways, "They continued steadfastly in the apostle's teaching (or doctrine) in fellowship, in breaking of bread, and in prayers". They continued steadfastly in these things, in the teaching of God's word.

Now then, we turn your thoughts to Acts, 2nd Chapter, and beginning we see that, "When the Day of Pentecost was

—3—

fully come there came a sound from Heaven as of a rushing, mighty wind, and it filled all the house wherein they were sitting, and there appeared unto them cloven tongues like as of fire and it sat upon each of them, and they began to speak with other tongues as the spirit gave them utterance. Now, when this was noised abroad the multitude came together," (and they remained together for that teaching.) "The multitude came together", they remained together for the instruction and teaching of God's word. We have here authority showing by example how the word of God was taught. Verse 14, "Peter, standing with the eleven, (they were right there together),"standing up with the eleven, lifted up his voice", and addressed the entire multitude. No segregating into classes. Those Elamites and various ones mentioned, strangers of Rome and from Phrygia, and so on, why, they were different nationalities of Jews who had come to Jerusalem.

We now turn to Acts 11:26. Here we find the teaching of God's word concerning a church of Jesus Christ and how it did in the beginning. "And when he had found him he brought him unto Antioch and it came to pass that a whole year they assembled themselves with the church, and taught much people and the disciples were called Christians first at Antioch." That would have been a good place to mention Sunday School assemblies. That would have been a fine place to tell how many they had at Sunday School, but they simply assembled as the church and not as a Sunday School. They came together and were taught the precious word of God. And notice how effective this was. "They taught much people", but they did not employ the modern day arrangement of classifying, grouping and grading the church. They did not have such. In Acts 20:7-8, we find the church of Christ at Troas came together upon the first day of the week. "They came together", they came together to worship God, and in the worship of God they had teaching. We find there that the apostle Paul did the teaching, no segregating into classes. They had approximately eight other teachers, but Paul at this time did all of the teaching as far as the context is concerned. They could have had classes. It could not be set aside on that occasion for a lack of teachers. They had plently, but they did not employ that. So Paul did the principal speaking or teaching on that occasion — no division into classes. In Acts 14:27-28 we have the church come together. 1 Cor. 16:1-2, we find they came together and they took up collection as part of their worship service. In Acts 15:25-31, we also find the church assembled.

Now then, friends, I am turning your attention to this side of the outline. Acts 2:1 through 41, we see that the multitude came together. One speaks at a time and that great address on that occasion was delivered by the apostle Peter. One assembly and one teacher, or male teacher, speaking at a time. Acts 3:12 — Here is another assembly. Peter is the speaker - no division into classes, no Sunday School, but they gathered together and were taught the word of God in multitudes. Acts 4:8 — Peter again preaching unto multitudes - no division into classes. Acts 7:2 — There Stephen said, "Men, brethren, and fathers, hearken unto me." A vast concourse of people. No division into classes. My friends, if a vast multitude could be argued as a necessity for organizing classes it is amazingly strange to me that the apostles did not think it necessary, for they never did such. In Acts 8:5-8, we have Phillip preaching -no division into classes. Acts 10:33-34, "Then Peter opened his mouth and spake unto them". No division into Classes. One assembly, one speaking at a time, and it was a man every time. Acts 11: 22-26, Barnabas and Saul did much teaching", but no division into classes. Acts 13:16, we find Paul preaching the word of God to a multitude, but no division into classes. Acts 15:7-13 — We find the church assembled, a great multitude, and on this occasion we have four preachers teaching, but they never divided that assembly into classes. Four of them, if you please. No women were allowed to speak. They learned in silence. There they gathered together, and four men did the teaching. How did they speak? One by one, one after the other, and all this, comes back to the command of God for it. 1 Cor. 14:31 — Here the apostle lays down the law or the commandment of the Lord showing the underlying fundamental reason why that there was not a variation to this rule in all assemblies in the church of Christ convened to worship and teach the word of the living God.

I shall now notice what Paul says unto the men who taught in those assemblies. "For ye may all prophesy (or teach) one by one that all may learn and all may be comforted." Here is the divine order laid down by the God of Heaven. God wanted the men to do the teaching, but he wanted everyone in their assemblies to hear all of the teachers on every occasion and he allowed only the men to do the teaching in the assemblies of the saints. God instructed them, "Ye may all prophesy (or teach) one by one", one after the other, just as I am affirming in my proposition, "one by one". Why? "That all may learn". All would learn from all of the teachers. That's God's divine order, that's God's plan, "and that all may be comforted." "Speak one by one."

Now then, the general rule is this: "For God is not the author of confusion, but of peace as in all churches (or assemblies) of the saints". That's why; because this is God's manner of avoiding confusion and edifying the church of the Lord Jesus Christ. This our Lord and Saviour has given by commandment through the apostle. God is not the author of confusion but of peace. He wants men to speak one by one unto all. All the church that assembles, that all may learn and all may be comforted. Thus, this shows that they did not have classified assemblies, and when this is followed they could not have it. Furthermore, it was not necessary. Furthermore, we see they would be edified and comforted by all of the teachers who taught by the authority of our Lord, Jesus Christ. This is the command of our Lord and Master.

Now then, with that much before us, I wish to turn to Phil. 4:9. Paul says, "those things which ye have both learned and received and heard and seen in me, do, and the God of peace shall be with you." Now, we have seen Paul in Acts 20 — he did all the teaching. In Acts 15 he was one of four teachers, and in all of these great examples; this host of examples, of churches or assemblies convened to be taught the word of God, one man taught at a time in harmony with God's divine plan for eliminating confusion and edifying all assemblies of the church. I defy any man to show a better plan. Now then we have learned and received and heard and seen these things in the apostles. That's what we're doing. That will bring unity on the teaching question, and under such a system as this in just a few years during the lifetime of the apostle Paul, he said that the gospel had been preached in all the world; had gone throughout all the kingdom, no doubt the Roman Empire, Thus showing how that God's plan will work when men work according to God's plan. Beloved, it is hard to get people now to go according to God's plan in anything.

Now then we turn and read from 1 Cor. 4:17 — This not only held for Corinth, but Paul said "in all churches". Let us read. "For this cause have I sent unto you Timotheus, who is my beloved son, and faithful in the Lord, who shall bring you into remembrance of my ways, which be in Christ, as I teach everywhere in every church." Yes, the apostle Paul said, Timothy will make known unto you these things and " may ways which be in Christ, as I teach everywhere in every church." Paul taught the same thing on the Lord's supper, the same thing on every other thing in every church, and he taught the same thing about teaching in every congregation. He'll make known all my ways unto you, how to worship God in spirit and in truth. And so we find, Acts 2:36-39, when unbelievers were taught the word of God; no division into classes, and one man speaking to them at a time. 1 Cor. 14:23-25, we find that when saved and unsaved people gathered together they were taught as Paul said, by men who spoke one by one to all. In Acts 20:7 where Christians assembled, no division into classes, to be taught the word of the Lord. Therefore, I think in those three categories that will take mankind at large. Therefore, if they did that, there is no necessity of it today, and it is forbidden by the command of the Lord. Speak and teach one by one unto all.

Now then, God regulates the teaching service. 1 Cor. 14:27, "If any man speak in an unknown tongue, let it be by two or at the most by three, and that by course, and let one interpret." Yes, here are regulations on tongue speakers. If any man should come into our assemblies today, the rules and regulations that regulated those inspired tongue speakers would regulate uninspired tongue speakers today, the same as those rules and regulations regulated the prophets then, it regulated all teachers of God's word.

Now then, friends, we turn to verses 34-35. Paul in writing to the church, speaks to the prophets, "Let your women keep silence in the church, for it is not permitted unto them to speak." "Your wives," wives of the prophets, can't teach in the assemblies of the church or saints. Why? Why, the apostle goes on to say, "if they will learn anything let them ask their husbands at home, for it is a shame for a woman to speak in the church." That is the underlying principle of the whole thing. That's why prophets' wives couldn't teach. That's why no woman could teach in the assemblies of the church. Because, "it is a shame for a woman to speak in the church." That's what Paul says.

Verse 37, "If any man think himself to be a prophet or spiritual let him acknowledge that the things that I write are the commandments of the Lord." These are God's commandments — of the Lord. "If any man be ignorant, let him be ignorant." If any man will not receive this teaching, will not have it, why then let him go. But if he will be ignorant, won't have it, you can't do anything with him. Those things the Lord has set forth.

Now then, we shall turn and read just a little more from the precious word of God. 1 Tim. 2:11-12 — I would like to read from 1 Tim. 1:3 — Paul said, I left you at a certain place to "charge some that they teach no other doctrine." Now then, we are going to see what that doctrine is. "Let" (that is the force of a commandment)," Let the woman learn in silence with all subjection." Where? Where is the woman to learn in silence with all subjection? Somewhere, where the word of God is being taught. It certainly isn't in the home. All right. "But I suffer not a woman to teach." Where is it? Paul said. "It is a shame for woman to speak in the church." The word "church" there is used in the sense of assemblies. "I suffer not a woman to teach." What else do you not suffer, Paul? "Nor (I don't allow this either) to usurp authority over the man." He doesn't allow that either. What else do you want her to do, Paul? "But to be in silence." Where is she to be in silence? Paul says, "For it is a shame for a woman to speak (that is, to teach) in the church," speak as the prophets (or men) were teaching; that is forbidden. That is what the apostle Paul is talking about. She is not allowed to address any assemblies of the church. She cannot do that. The Lord had no woman among the apostles. He did not send out women evangelists, nor elders; nor did he set forth them in the church to rule the body of the Lord Jesus Christ. But they are to come together and they are to learn in silence as God's word directs, and we find that men are to do this teaching.

I want you to remember God's divine order of eliminating confusion and edifying the church. Men have come along in the 19th Century and they think that they have found something that's wonderful, and they are exalting the wisdom of men above the wisdom of God. They cannot pass. God's word shall stand. "For ye may all prophesy, one by one, that all may learn and all may be comforted." This is the law of the Lord and Saviour, Jesus Christ. Col. 2:5 — "Though I be absent in the

—8—

flesh, yet am I with you in the spirit, joying and beholding your order," and he gave the order. "Let all things be done decently and in order." This the apostle laid down. This is the apostle's order, and I have obligated myself to prove this by the scriptures, and friends, my proposition is sustained.

Porter's First Speech
Dec. 4, 1951

Brethren, Moderators, Brother Abercrombie, Ladies and Gentlemen:

It affords me pleasure to be before you at this time to reply to the speech to which you have listened as made by my opponent. He is endeavoring to sustain the proposition which has been read and, at least, defined in part, that "the scriptures teach that when people come together to be taught by the church they should remain in one group, and the teaching should be done by men only, one speaking at a time to the assembly." He told us that by "teaching" he meant that the New Testament teaches by command and example, and that by "groups" he meant that there should not be any segregating, or taking some groups away from other groups, or from the other group. And I would like to have just a little more about the meaning of that part of the proposition that says that teaching should be done in one group; that is, they should remain in one group. I want to know tonight, Cecil, if that means that they must remain in one group. Does the word "should" in this proposition have the significance of "must"? Do you mean that they must remain in one group under the penalty of the eternal fires of hell? Just what do you mean by saying they "should" remain in one group? Do you mean that they must remain in one group, and if they do not remain in one group, that hell is to be their final destiny? Now, I think that we have a right to demand that you answer that and tell us in your next speech so that we can get into this matter. But before I reply to the arguments made, I want to present to my opponent some questions. I'll hand him one copy of them so that he can read them as I read them to the audience.

1. What characteristics must an assembly possess in order to constitute a church assembly?

2. Is a Bible class, or a Sunday School class, a church assembly?

3. Is it a sin to divide a church assembly?

4. How far must some be removed from the others before an assembly becomes divided?

5. Are two things ever parallel in one point but not paralleled in other points?

6. Can two men scripturally preach from two radio sta-

tions operating on different kilocycles in separate room of the same building at the same time?

7. Can the church scripturally call together a special group for special training?

8. Can two groups from two different congregations scripturally meet in separate places for simultaneous teaching and worship?

Now, I shall expect Cecil to answer those in his next speech so that we can get into these matters and have time to thresh them out. I therefore shall be looking for some answers from my opponent regarding those particular points, because they cover some of the very things at issue in this debate tonight.

Going then to the speech that he made, he mentioned the fact that this is a serious question, that the church of the Lord Jesus Christ is divided over it, and he talked about there being strength in unity; to all of which, of course, I give my full accord.

Then he referred to the 17th chapter of John, verses 20-21, in which Jesus prayed that "they all might be one," and on the heels of that statement he said, "Our practice has not divided the church, but classifying, segregating into classes, or groups, with women teachers, has divided the church." Therefore, he puts the responsibility of division upon me and those who stand with me - that the division has not come over his practice, he says, but it has come over our practice. Well, I am going to turn that thing around just a little bit and let Cecil have hold of another part of it. Not only is there division in the church over this particular point, but there is also division in the church over the communion cup question. There is a group of brethren, a small group of radicals, who claim that in the communion service you must use only one drinking vessel; and Brother Abercrombie will say that they can scripturally do that if they want to. I challenge him to say otherwise. But doesn't Cecil use a plurality of communion cups and over debate with those brethren about the communion cups? It has not been but just a very short time since he was engaged in a debate of that kind down in Texas somewhere, I believe it was, and so there is division over the plurality of communion cups, and those brethren can come to Cecil and say, "Now, Cecil, the church is divided over this matter." They will say, "The church is not divided over our practice. Cecil will admit that we can use one drinking vessel if we want to; therefore, the church is divided over the practice of Cecil and his brethren who have a plurality of cups." All right, Cecil, if you are insisting and arguing that I must give up our classes because you say the church is divided over them, then upon the same ground and from the same standpoint, you must throw away your plurality of cups and take your stand with the brethren who advocate the one literal drinking vessel. Cecil, you are occupying a position that cannot be maintained. You are entirely inconsistent, even more so than the "one-cup" brethren. You are in a position between the two; and for you to be consistent you must either take your stand with us upon the class question, or you must take your stand with the "one-cup" brethren on the drinking vessel question. You can't occupy your position tonight as one in between the two and maintain it by any strength of argument, or any sort of reason or logic, whatsoever. It can't be done. Well, do we ever call Cecil's practice in question? Certainly so! I'm telling you tonight, my friends, that the church is divided over his practice right in this connection tonight, simply because Cecil and his brethren have made a law where God has not made one. When they say the church must remain in an undivided assembly — that the church must remain in one group in order for teaching to be done — they are making a law that the apostle Paul never did make and that no inspired man over made, that the God of heaven never revealed in all his book divine. And that law which he has made is responsible for the division. If Cecil wants to do all of his teaching to one group, in one assembly, I have no objection. I would not fall out with him in the least, just as he would not fall out with Brother Ervin Waters and others who contend for one literal drinking vessel. But when Cecil makes a law that God has not made and says that all teaching must be done in one group, that the Church must remain in an undivided assembly, when God has said nothing of the kind, then I object ot that. He says those "literal drinking cup" brethren have made a law where God hasn't made it when they say that "you must have one drinking vessel." They have made the same kind of law that Cecil has made when he says that "the church must remain an undivided assembly." So we pass.

He came to his chart then, and referred to teaching when the church assembles, and what God's way is. 1 Cor. 14:40 —

that God said, "Let everything be done decently and in order." And he said in some things God has not been specific, but he has been specific about teaching. Yes, he has been specific about teaching, so far as the thing to be taught is concerned. God has specified that men must teach the truth. God has condemned the teaching of error. But God has not been specific about methods of teaching. Not any more than he has been specific about some other things to which your attention has already been called. If God has been specific about teaching, if what God has said covers the whole thing along that line, when Cecil, I want to know where you have read, in any of these assemblies you have listed on your board, where Paul, Peter, James, or John or any other concerned over had a radio program. Come on, tell us about it. Remember, God has been specific about teaching. God has specified what you can do and what you can't do. You insist that God has given all the details about the matter with respect to the method or manner of teaching. All right then, where do you get your details for radio preaching? Where do you get your details for the singing schools taught by the churches with which you stand identified? Where do you get those details in God's book if God has been specific about all those matters? There'll be more about that later on.

In Matthew 28:19, we read, "Go ye therefore and teach all nations," or "make disciples of all nations" (as the Revised Version reads); and Cecil says there is no limit as to how we go but teaching is restricted. Yes, as I have already mentioned, we are restricted as to *what we teach,* but we are not restricted as to how we teach. The methods by which the teaching is done are not revealed or outlined in God's book. If so, by what New Testament authority, Cecil, do you get your chart that you have on the board tonight, or that you have on the wall? Oh, it's on the board, too, isn't it? All right, by what method, by what New Testament authority, by what New Testament passage, by what assembly listed on this chart, do you get any authority for the chart, if God has been so specific about the whole thing?

He called our attention to some of the assemblies. First, Matt. 18:20 "Where two or three are gathered together in my name, there will I be in the midst of them." Cecil said where there are two or three, you could not have classes in an assembly that small. Well, I do not suppose any of my
—14—

brethren ever tried to. I have never heard of my brethren trying to have classes where there are only three assembled. I never have. If he knows of it, he knows of something I do not. I do not know of a case of that kind. But just because you could not have classes in an assembly that small, does that prove that all teaching, under all other circumstances, and in all other assemblies, and all other groups, must be done in one group or in one group or in one assembly? Not at all. That's Cecil's law. God didn't say a thing of the kind.

Heb. 10:25 "Forsake not the assembling of yourselves together." And here they had an assembly. No body disputes that. James 2:2 speaks about those coming into your assembly, and no one disputes that there were assemblies, and there have been assemblies throughout the years, and we have assemblies all over the world today. But he says that not one of these verses tells you anything about classifying. Well, does either one of them tell anything about radio preaching? Does any one of them tell anything about having a plurality of communion cups in the Lord's supper? Does either of these tell anything about using a chart to get your argument before an audience? Does either one of these assemblies say one word about teaching a singing school by the church? No, not a thing, and yet Cecil can see all these other things in them without any details, but when it comes to a matter of class teaching, he's got to have every detail specifically mentioned.

Then to the approved examples. Matt. 16:18; "Upon this rock I will build my church." He said the church here was the thing that should do the teaching. Nobody disputes that. Acts 2:42: "They continued steadfastly in the apostles' doctrine, fellowship, breaking of bread, and in prayers." No one disputes that.

Acts 2:1-4, "The multitude came together (and remained together) and Peter addressed the entire multitude." In verse 14, he said that Peter stood up and addressed the entire multitude. So he says in Acts, 2nd chapter, there was one speaker and one assembly. The entire multitude was addressed by Peter. Yes, beginning with verse 14 we are told that Peter addressed the entire multitude, but why did you skip so far, Cecil? Why did you start with the first of the chapter and then skip all the intervening verses to get down to verse 14, and down to that which speaks about Peter's addressing the whole multitude? He brought this passage up two or three times. So I'll just deal with it now. The 2nd chapter of Acts, the first four verses, teaches about the outpouring of the Holy Spirit, and "they began to speak with other tongues as the spirit gave them utterance." And then we are informed in the fifth verse that "there were dwelling in Jerusalem Jews, devout men, out of every nation under heaven." Now, this is before we get to verse 14. Cecil skipped all of this. "Now when this was noised abroad, the multitude came together, and were confounded, because that every man heard then speak in his own language, and they were all amazed and marvelled, saying one to another, "Behold are not all those which speak Galileans?" It didn't say, "Are not all these who spoke Galileans", but "are not all these which *speak* (present tense) Galileans?" "And how *hear we* every man in our own tongue, wherein we were born?" Not *heard*, but *hear*. "How hear we every man in our own tongue, wherein we were born?" And then in verses 9 to 11, Luke gives a list of the places from which they came, and the last of verse 11 said, "We do hear them speak in our tongues the wonderful works of God." Not *"We heard them speak in our tongues"*, but *"We do hear them speak"*, using the present tense. So there were a number of languages, there were a number of tongues, represented there, and people in that multitude were already divided from the standpoint of language. They were addressed in their own tongue in which they were born, and there were a number of speakers there, and how does he know that some man was not addressing one group of men in their language, another, another group in their language, and so on and on? He simply assumed the whole thing. So the very passage he used to prove that there is no division upsets his whole point along that line. He passed all of that by in silence and skipped down to verse 14 in order to get Peter addressing the whole multitude.

He came to Acts 11:26, "they assembled with the church." Oh, he said there is where they were called Christians first at Antioch, and this would have been a good place to have mentioned the Sunday School. It wouldn't have been any better place to mention the Sunday School, Cecil, than it would have been to mention the Singing School. It would have been just as good a place to have mentioned the radio program. It is just as good a place to have mentioned the chart, like the one you have on the board here, and yet none of these things is mentioned in that passage. Cecil argues that because the Bible classes, or what he calls the Sunday School, is not mentioned in that verse, that disproves the right to use any such method. Well, upon the very same basis it proves it is wrong to preach over a radio. It proves it is wrong to use a blackboard or a chart in his sermons. It proves it is wrong to teach a singing school, because none of these things is mentioned there. He wants the other man to give every detail for everything that he does, but will Cecil give the details of his practice? No. Absolutely not. You watch and see if he does.

By the way, Cecil, I wonder if there is anything said there about an arranged or pre-arranged debate between two of the preachers of that time. Where do you get the details of that? Cecil is engaging in a religious discussion, a religious debate, here. I want to know, Cecil, if you can find in any passage of God's book, if you can find anywhere in any assembly to which you referred, an arrangement of the details of a debate. Now, for example, in the first place, where Paul challenged Peter for a debate; in the second place, where they signed propositions; and in the third place, where they spoke alternately for thirty minutes; and then where James and John served as their moderators. I want you to find that. You are now engaging in that sort of thing here tonight. Where can you get the details of it in God's book? It just isn't there; and yet Cecil has no compunction of conscience about that.

He came to Acts 20:7-8, "They came together," and they had teaching and no segregating; and he said that they could have had the classes. Yes, they could have had a singing school, too, but they didn't as far as the record goes.

Then to Acts 14:27-28, and he gave this as an assembly. This was an assembly that was called together for the purpose of making a report on missionary work and not for the purpose of teaching the church. He has the wrong assembly. Then to Acts 15:25-31, "the church assembled". And Acts 2:1-41, he gets back to that again. An assembly in Acts 3:12 where Peter was the speaker. Yes, in that assembly they came together out of curiosity, because a man had been healed of his lameness. It does not say they came together to be taught. In Acts 4:8 where Peter preached to the multitude, and that was where he was called before the Jewish council and given a trial. In Acts 7:2, the case of Stephen, and that was where Stephen came before the council to be tried, and actually was condemned to die, and lost his life as a result of it. He has the wrong kind of assemblies in all those. He was going to make the assembly simply mean *the people coming together for the purpose of being taught.* Acts 8:5-6 — he finds another assembly. In Acts 10:33-34 — Peter preached to Cornelius and his household. Acts 11:22-26, he goes back to that — Barnabas and Saul at Antioch. Acts 13:26, where Paul did some preaching. He didn't make any arguments on this. He merely referred to them. Acts 15:7 — there were four preachers, but they never divided into classes. No women were allowed to speak. Well, that does not harmonize with your law in 1 Cor. 14. If you think 1 Cor. 14 covers every teaching program of the church. then you have a direct conflict here, because the law laid down in 1 Cor. 14:31 says, "Let it be by two or *at the most by three,*" with tongue speakers and prophets. It said they may prophesy "two or three," and so he gets three as the maximum in that case, but here he has four. So he admits 1 Cor. 14 doesn't cover every teaching program of the church.

Then I come to the command. 1 Cor. 14:31 (all of these he has listed on his chart). "Ye may all prophesy one by one, that all may learn," and the general rule was that God was not the author of confusion. And he turned around and said that here the apostle Paul said, "Ye must speak one by one unto all, that all may learn, and all may be comforted." Cecil is noted for a misquotation of that passage. *Cecil is noted for a misquotation of that passage.* The passage does not say the thing that Cecil quotes it to say over and over in his debates. I have heard him say it a number of times, and perhaps will say it a number of times before he gets through with this debate, that Paul said, "Ye must teach one by one *unto all,* that all may learn, and all may be comforted." It doesn't say any such thing, does it, Cecil? Didn't you add the expression, "unto all"? Is that in there or did you just read it in there? You must "teach one by one *to all*"? "To all". Well, we'll wait and see more about that.

Philippians 4:9 — "The things", Paul said, "ye have heard and seen in me, that do", and he said in Acts 20 we saw where he did all the teaching. In Acts 14:27-28 he was one of four teachers, and therefore Cecil reasons that you are not allowed to do anything that you didn't see and hear Paul do. Now, where did you see and hear Paul preach on a radio program? Huh? Now where did you ever read or see anything about Paul's using a chart for his teaching? Anything of that kind?

—18—

Not any of these things is mentioned here that they had seen and heard in him. How are you going to get those things, Cecil? But he ways this is the rule, now, in all the churches.

In 1 Cor. 4:17, Paul speaks about "may ways, as I teach everywhere in every church." I wonder if I mis-read that. Let me turn and read that passage again. 1 Cor. 4:17. I thought I knew what it said, but I want to be sure. Maybe I am wrong about the whole thing. 1 Cor. 4:17 — "For this cause have I sent unto you Timotheus, who is my beloved son, and faithful in the Lord, who shall bring you into remembrance of *my ways.*" What? Am I reading that right? "Who shall bring you into remembrance of *my ways.*" Now, Paul, you're wrong about that. You used "ways" there in the plural number. "My ways", not "my way", but "my ways". I am afraid you have the wrong passage, Cecil.

On his chart again he brings up down here (pointing to chart) Acts 2:36-39 — the unbelievers. 1 Cor. 14:23-25, the saved and the unsaved; Acts 20:7, the Christians. He said that in none of these any segregation or division. Well, we have already shown he is wrong about one of them to start with; and so that takes care of his whole argument on that. But just granting that there is no mention of any division of any kind, or any segregation, or any groups of any nature, in any of these assemblies mentioned here, then we'll just turn it around again and ask him if there is any radio preaching in any of them. Was there any singing schools taught in any of them? Now, those you stand with, Cecil, teach singing schools; and they are taught *with the church,* and they are taught *for the church,* and they are taught *by the church. The church does the teaching.* It is done *by* the church, it is done *for* the church, it is done *with* the church, among brethren with whom he stands identified. Yet they have no details of it in God's book. Not one of these assemblies mentions anything of the kind. And yet Cecil can find authority for that. But he can't find any authority for class teaching.

Now, regarding Sunday School, I have no objection to the term, "Sunday School", as long as you use it simply to mean teaching that is done on Sunday, just as you might refer to teaching done on Monday as a "Monday School", or teaching done on Friday as a "Friday School", or something of that kind. But if by that Cecil means a separate, distinct orgainzation or institution in addition to the church, then I am utterly opposed to anything of that kind. Well, certainly I am, if that's what he's meaning by the term "Sunday School," if that is all he has in mind by it, why, we could just shake hands and close the debate, if that's all he means by it. But if he uses the term simply to mean teaching that is done on Sunday and call that a Sunday School because of that fact, well, then, I am not going to object to the term. We'll just let it go at that point and see what he might have to say about it.

1 Cor. 14:35, in the 27th verse tongue speakers spoke by course, one at a time. Verses 34-35, the women were not permitted to speak, but were told "if they would learn anything, let them ask their husbands at home, for it is a shame for women to speak in the church." Cecil, I want to know tonight, is this law laid down in 1 Cor. 14 unlimited? Do you make an unlimited, universal law of this, or do you permit some exceptions of some kind to creep in somewhere? If not, then, since Paul said "if they will learn *anything*," let them ask their husbands at home." Now, is that unlimited? "if they will *learn anything*. Is that unlimited? If so, they could not even listen to another prophet give a revelation, because they might learn something. They would have to go home before that happened. For "if they would learn anything, ask their husbands." "If they learn anything." So there must be some limitations placed upon the learning and the silence and the speaking as revealed to us in that: and that will be more fully developed as we go along into the debate.

Verse 37, he tells us that these "are the commandments of the Lord." And he brought in connection with that 1 Tim. 1:3, where Paul admonished that "they teach no other doctrine." Then he came to 1 Tim. 2:11-12 in which Paul said, "Let the women learn in silence with all subjection, for I suffer not a woman to teach." Cecil said that means, "I suffer her not to teach in the church." Did he say so, Cecil? Or are you reading something into it? Did it say so? "I suffer not a woman to teach." He said that means "in the church." All right. "Nor to usurp authority over the man." Does that mean "in the church", too? Now are you going to make one of them mean "in the church" and let the other mean something else? "I suffer not a woman to teach, nor to usurp authority over the man". He says the "teach" means teach *in the church*. She can teach anywhere else, but not in the church assembly. All right,

—20—

in the same passage, "Nor to usurp authority over the man". *So she can usurp authority over the man anywhere else except in the church.* She does not have to be in subjection to the husband, or to the man, anywhere except in the church, you see, because all this has to do with church duties, according to Cecil.

He said also there were no women among the prophets. Huh? What about Phillip's daughters over in Acts 21:8-9? It said they prophesied. They had some prophetesses over there. There were some women prophets in Acts 21:8-9. Phillip had daughters that prophesied. Cecil said there was none among them. That is between you and the book of God about that. I didn't put it in there, and I'm not going to let you take it out.

God's order of eliminating confusion, he said, is this laid down here that one spoke at a time. "God is not the author of confusion, but of peace, in all the churches of the saints". And God gave an order on teaching. Yes, here's God's order, a God given order on teaching, and he said that order is to speak one by one. Nobody denies that. I have never seen any of my brethren teach contrary to that principle. In all of our assemblies, we have only one teacher to one group, one teacher to one assembly. We never have two teachers speaking at the same time in one group, or in one assembly, Cecil. I've never seen it that way, and my brethren do not violate God's law laid down in 1 Cor. 14:31, because that contemplated one speaker to one assembly, one speaker to one group, Now, the thing that is wrong with your whole set-up here is that you are putting a law in there that is not there — that God declares and *God requires that they must remain in one group, they must remain an undivided assembly* to be taught. God nowhere said that. That is not found in God's order. That is in Cecil's order. God's order doesn't cover that at all. And since your're having trouble with the order, why, we might give you Acts 2:42 in which Luke said, "They continued steadfastly in the apostle's doctrine, in fellowship, in breaking of bread, and in prayers." There is a group of anti-class brethren, being led in particular by Brother J. D. Phillips, who insists upon that particular order being followed. You must first have the apostles' doctrine, then you must have the fellowship, the breaking of bread, and finally prayers. That you must follow that order, or you're anti-scriptural, and you are digressive, and Cecil would not be willing to accept their position on that at all. Yet he would say, no doubt, that they could do it that way if they wanted to, provided they don't make a law that God hasn't made and say that I must do it that way. Well, he's in the very same predicament that James Douglas Phillips is in on his order of worship. He is in the very same predicament that Ervin Waters is with respect to his literal drinking cup. All three of them are making laws where God didn't make them. Thank you, Ladies and Gentlemen.

Abercrombie's Second Speech
Dec. 4, 1951

Ladies and Gentlemen, Fellow Moderators, Worthy Opponent:

I'm happy to stand before you once more to continue my affirmative concerning God's order of teaching the word when the church assembles. Let us now notice again the proposition which I am affirming: "The Scriptures Teach that When People Come Together to be Taught by the Church, They Should Remain on One Group, and the Teaching Should be Done by Men Only, One Speaking at a Time to the Assembly".

Brother Porter has come here and virtually acknowledged the scriptures which I have offered as being the truth. He knows that it is the truth, and he cannot deny it. And all that he can do is merely quibble around on extraneous matter, things that have nothing to do whatsoever with the proposition — not in the proposition at all, and he wants to bring up a new issue; or several of them, and debate them. Now, when Brother Porter and I differ on something else and he charges that what I'm doing is sinful, then we'll be glad to devote another week to find out whether singing schools are scriptural or not, and if he charges that radio preaching is sinful, I'll be glad to come to the defense of that — the use I make of that, in another discussion, but that has nothing to do whatsoever with what we do when the church comes together to be taught, what the scriptures teach about that. Now, it might be a sin to preach over the radio, but that is not the subject under consideration. Now, that's all that he has to present, that's the whole thing that he's trying to confuse the people and get their minds off of my proposition. He knows better than try to grapple with these scriptures, because he can't touch them. He just floundered around on them a while ago, virtually admitted every one of them. Why, he knows that he can't do one thing with it. Then he wants to get me into a debate with him about the cup question. As far as I know we agree on that, but if we disagree on that, I'll debate him on that next week. He does not believe the cuppers are right, he says they're sinful. He said he debates them all over the country, he said I did. He debates them all over the country. He believes they're just as wrong as I do. All of that is beside the point. That's not the subject of this discussion. *I am here not to prove my practice by bringing up something that maybe Brother Porter's doing.*

I'm here to prove by the word of God. Now all that is junk that he mentioned. It might be wrong, or it might not be wrong, as far as I'm concerned. It does not make a bit of difference. All that I am here to discuss is the proposition that I signed. That's what I am here to debate.

All right. "The scriptures teach". By the word of God, it sets forth just what my proposition says. Now then, Brother Porter had something to say about "should", and he wanted to know if that was a law that was going to send people to hell. I suppose Brother Porter wanted to get a little prejudice stirred up by that. It does not make any difference to me whether people believe the word of God or not, as far as that's concerned, but it is my duty to preach it, and if they don't receive it, then I can't help that. God's word must be believed, it must be obeyed. But now he talked about the "must" there. I want to ask Brother Porter to present to this people; *Must those teachers that Paul mentioned there in the church, must they speak as Paul said, or could they do it just any old way?* Could they do it as you do? "Must." I want to see how you stand on the "must." *Must* they do that as Paul said? Talk about *must!* I didn't put any "must" in there. Paul put there. Yes sir. We'll see how he stands on it. *"Must" those men speak as Paul said, or can they do it your way?* All right, we'll hear more maybe, about that later.

The responsibility of the division certainly rests on his shoulders. When the Sunday School mania came along the world went after it. Denominations took it in, and it was not long until the Church of Christ, began to want that thing, and so it went in, in over the protests of godly brethren, protesting it. *Usurped authority over them.* Yes, went right on in. Makes no difference. *They wanted it just like every other innovation. That's how it got in.* The responsibility of the division rests on his shoulders. He has broken, flagrantly violated the law of the Lord. By what Paul said here in the 31st verse, that will outlaw his method, his agency, organization through which it's done. He has an organization to do teaching. He talked about the Sunday School as a *method* of teaching. *It is an organization through which to do teaching. It's like a missionary society; is an organization through which to do teaching.* So we find that's what he has. The division rests on him. The Church of Christ wasn't divided over this question until his brethren put it in. They put it in over our protests, the protests of our fathers in the faith. They're the ones who divided the church over it. They set at naught these scriptures, they ignored all the examples. They threw them out the window. The commands of the Lord didn't amount to anything, and then they come back and say, "he says must", and that is what's divided. The apostle Paul has put it there. *Must those men speak as Paul said, and must those women learn in silence as he said?* No, they don't have to do that! They can teach! They can teach some of those assemblies, they can teach assemblies of the church!

All right. "Cup question" — one vessel. He knows that we can't unite with them on the vessel, we can't unite with them at all on that. All of this is just irrelevant matter entirely. You've got to believe that that is the Lord's cup — *the vessel,* otherwise they won't fellowship you. There is not unity with them on that. *The cases are not parallel at all.*

Then he say, "Cecil made a law". No sir, Cecil hasn't made any law. I have read to you what the Law of the Spirit is. "For ye may all prophesy one by one (that means to teach one by one) that all may learn and all may be comforted". Yes, that's the law and Paul says in verse 37, "if any man thinks himself to be a prophet or spiritual, let him acknowledge that the things that I write unto you are the commandments of the Lord." Now he said I said that. He said that Cecil made a law here. Paul said, *"I want you to acknowledge that what I write is the commandments of the Lord."* He said, "Cecil wrote that." I'm not that old, Brother Porter. I may look pretty old, but I'm not. Paul wrote that. You know he did, and why don't you acknowledge it? Paul wrote for the men to *speak one by one. Must they speak that way? If they did, how would then, they divide up into classes?* How could the classes be taught? They spoke *one by one to all.* Divide them up into various classes and scatter them out, they wouldn't get any teaching. One group might, the rest of them wouldn't because they spoke one by one-by course. That's what the Lord said. You'll have to do better than that.

Now, I want to analyze this passage of scriptures just a little more. "For ye may all prophesy (that is, teach) *one by one that all may learn and all may be comforted."* Now, that's exactly how it reads. If I didn't read it that way I didn't intend to read it otherwise. Now that's the way it reads.

All right, let us just notice, friends, brethren. All we're after is to learn what the scriptures teach. I don't care what it teaches. I just want to know what it does teach and do that. If it teaches his practice, that's well and good. I'll take it. "For ye may all prophesy (teach) one by one."

Now notice verse 33. — "God is not the author of confusion but of peace as in all churches of the saints." Churches there is used in the sense of assemblies. He knows that. He didn't deny it. Now then, "God is not the author of confusion but of peace as in all churches (or assemblies) of the saints." *In all of them*. Now, this holds in *all assemblies of the saints*. What holds? God's order of doing away with confusion and edifying the church, that's what. "Speak one by one." Brother Porter has been arguing here that no specifications, no restrictions have been given, *no "how"*, no "how" to teach the word of God. That's his argument. " The Lord said teach, and didn't say how." Now, I am wondering why Paul wasted this whole chapter almost in telling them how to teach in the assemblies. I wonder why he wasted this page. It doesn't go for anything with Brother Porter. It doesn't mean a thing to him. Not one thing, because he just said teach, a broad, general term. Just teach any way you please. No wonder people started missionary societies, Sunday schools, according to his theory! Friends, the apostle Paul has certainly laid down restrictions here, and that's what we're dealing with — the word of the Living God. "For ye may all teach (or Prophesy) one by one that all may learn" — now notice — as they did teach the church one at a time, one by one, *that all may learn, that is, all would learn from all the teachers and all may be comforted, that all may be comforted by all the teachers that taught in that assembly*. Now, that is what the Lord laid down. That is His law of order and the Lord has put that in as a *must*. "Ye may all prophesy one by one that all may learn and all may be comforted", and the spirit of the prophets are subject to the prophets. "God is not the author of confusion, but of peace as in all (assemblies) churches of the saints." Now then, we'll deal with the other portion of that in just a few minutes.

I've already taken care of the thoughts that he presented about preaching over the radio. He believes that that's scriptural. I believe that it is scriptural. It does not violate any principle that I am contending for tonight. He doesn't believe it is sinful, but if he believes it is sinful and he charges that I am committing a sin in preaching over the radio, I guess we could debate that about Saturday night of next week, but when he says that I'm committing a sin in that, he's committing a sin too.

Be that as it may. Maybe we're both sinning in it! What does it matter about such a thing as that? Not a straw! We're here to discuss what the church does when it comes together. Another thing about that, my friends, Paul couldn't have preached over a radio if he had wanted to, but he could have organized Brother Porter's classes, he could have had that, but he couldn't have preached over a radio if he had wanted to. That was a thing of future invention, just like a telephone. He could have had the classes, though, but for some reason or another he overlooked such an essential thing!

As far as Brother Porter and his brethren are concerned, then, he said there is no "how" given and if that is true, why do you oppose the missionary society, if there is no "how" given to teach the word of God, to preach the gospel? Why do you oppose that? Yet he opposes it. *Just how, my friends, he can stretch Matt. 28:19 to include his Sunday School organization and then rule out the missionary society is beyond me!* That's something that he'll have to explain. Yes sir, my friends.

Matt. 18:20, he said none of his brethren ever tried to put a Sunday School in a church of two or three. I don't know, they have tried a lot of things. But you know they couldn't have it, to have a plurality of classes, of two or three. Analyze it. But there is authority for assembling, or an assembly of the church. It's modified by "in the name of the Lord". Come together in the name of the Lord to worship him or teach his word, and such like. If Porter charges that anything else that I do is sinful, we'll debate that.

Now we come to Acts, the 2nd chapter. He says, "Why skip to verse 14?" *You skipped from verse one to five.* What did you skip that for? I can't skip, but he can! All right, let's turn back there. We will turn to Acts, 2nd chapter, and let us see if he gets any comfort out of it. It is against him and he knows it. We've covered this ground before. "And when the day of Pentecost was fully come they were all with one accord in one place (the apostles), and suddenly there came a sound from Heaven as of a rushing mighty wind, and it filled all the house where they were sitting." They were all with one accord, now, in one place, the apostles all sitting there in one place together. "And there appeared unto them cloven tongues like as of fire, and it sat upon each of them; and they were all filled with the Holy Ghost and began to speak with other tongues *as the Spirit gave them utterance.*" Why did you overlook that? No wonder you skipped that verse. You know the Spirit does not want you to speak where you couldn't be understood. *But there they are together in one place,* and Brother Porter has twelve men all talking at the same time in one place. Talk about confusion! There it is. Put twelve men up here and let them all talk in a different tongue and see how much you get out of it. But now let us notice this thing. "There were dwelling at Jerusalem, Jews, devout men out of every nation under heaven. Now when this was noised abroad", what happened? *"The multitude came together."* I wonder who they were teaching over there, Brother Porter, when that was noised abroad after that had taken place, and who were they teaching then? After this was noised abroad, then the multitude came, and after that the multitude was taught and heard them teach. Who were they teaching in the first place? It was noised abroad that they were speaking in other tongues. Allright. "The multitude came together and were confounded, because that every man heard them speak in his own language." Now they came together, and they were still hearing some teaching but how did they speak? All at one time? They spoke like Peter did down there in verse 14. "Peter, standing up with the eleven, lifted up his voice." The rest of them were silent. Verse 4 says, *"they spoke as the Spirit gave them utterance".* The spirit taught tongue speakers to speak one at a time. And the Lord, over in 1 Cor. by the pen of Paul, wrote a regulation and restriction, and gave a commandment that those who did speak in tongues had to speak one at a time. At the beginning here we have a miraculous demonstration. This was the birthday of the Church of Christ. All of these men spoke in tongues, the context indicated, but later on we have the apostle Paul writing *a specific commandment* giving regulations on such tongues in the church, regulating it to two or three speaking in tongues in the assemblies. But here at the beginning it shows, that all of them did speak in tongues, but how did they do it? *"As the Spirit gave them utterance." The multitude came together.*

Now Brother Porter would have you believe that — he says they were divided, they were divided in language. Divided in language! Why, you don't divide the Sunday School up according to language. Do you? You just have one speech, don't you? That doesn't fit you class system, does it? Why, of course not, but now then, were those languages of people segregated into different groups to be taught? Certainly not. It says *they came together. Now you get them apart.* You're the man that knows how to classify. Classify! Get them segregated. Get them off in classes, if you please. "The multitude came together." "They were all amazed and marvelled, saying one to another, 'Behold, are not all these which speak Galileans'?" It indicates there was a plurality of speakers, but were they separated? Verse 14 shows the apostles were still right together. "Peter, standing up with the eleven, lifted up his voice and the congregation was all together. They came together and remained together, but now he would have you think that these murderers of the Lord would be so docile, and so humble that they would allow the apostles to classify them to teach them, and then probably come back together again and let Peter preach to them, to simulate what he does in his class system in Lord's Day worship. *Why, it's ridiculous!*

"Parthians, Medes, Elamites, dwellers in Mesopotamia, Judaea, Cappadocia, Pontus, Asia, Phrygia", and so on, about 17 different nationalities, or something like that. Different languages. "They were all amazed, were in doubt saying one to another, 'What meaneth this?' Others mocking, said, 'These men are full of new wine'. Peter, standing up with the eleven, lifted up his voice and said unto them, 'Ye men of Judaea and all ye that dwelleth in Jerusalem, be this known unto you and hearken to my words'," and he explained the whole situation. My beloved friends, he'll never find a Sunday School there.

So now we shall pass on. He asked me how do I know there were not classes there? I'm anxious to know how he knows they are there. I know they weren't there because it says they came together. We never see any segregation. They didn't do that. And then Peter addressed the multitude. That's why I say they were not there. I could find a thousand different classifications in this multitude here. There might be some different tongues here (in this assembly) for all I know. "Bald heads", and those who haven't hair on their head — classify them that way. "old and young," "male and female," but they did not classify in the apostolic days to teach the word of God.

They taught them in general church assemblies. He knows that. Acts 11:26 — I showed from that, that they came together and they taught much people the word of the Lord. The church came together. Taught them without Sunday School, without all these superhumanly devised inventions of the modern day. They taught as the apostles gave here, by command of the Lord, 1 Cor. 14:31. All of these examples are corroborative evidence concerning the command of God that I have produced in affirmation of this proposition tonight, and he hasn't phased one of them. He merely picked out a few things to quibble over as he passed along very rapidly. Then he charged unjustly that I want other men or the other man to give all the details on everything when he knows that I said that all the details were not given on some things, but that the thing that we are discussing here, God has given details on.

Just an illustration: God told us to take up a collection, or to contribute of our means. He didn't say whether to put it in a hat, put it in a box as you come in, or lay it on a table. There is some liberty there. But we must do it, and where God has not given specific details concerning such a thing as that we are at liberty to do it the best way we think fit. But has God left us on the teaching subject under that head? I say he has not. My proposition is sustained by a host of examples and by command of the Lord and Saviour, Jesus Christ, and he tries to contend that he obeys this in his classes. Yes, he applies this to his classes! I want you to notice his teaching. All that assembled were to hear the teachers and be comforted and modified and they would if they taught one by one. Now then, I want you to see the mess he has gotten himself into in applying this to his classes. *He is going to have to rotate his teachers to every class in order for all the people to hear all the teachers. Going to get women teaching men after all!* Yes sir. Here Paul showed that the church heard all the teachers, and he says that we do this in our class system. He's going now to, after he segregates and divides up and does the teaching, now he is going to have to continue to do the teaching by *rotating the teachers* to all the people so all the people will hear all the teachers. Such a mess! He knows that he doesn't do that. He can't do it. According to his own doctrine he wouldn't let a woman teach a man. Paul down here says that she can't teach anybody, wherever that applies. "It is a shame for a woman to speak (or teach) in the church". No sir, Paul put her out of the teaching in church assemblies.

All right. 1 Cor. 14:31 — there the apostle says, "Speak one by one that all may learn and all may be comforted". Now think of that, friends. That's a command. The apostle didn't just put that in to hear himself talk or to waste the time of the brethren at Corinth, and in every place where he went. Now then, let us analyze that again. Here the apostle said, "Speak one by one that all may learn and all may be comforted." You can see in that, that all assembled were to hear all of the teachers that taught in that assembly. He does not follow it. His class system does not in any way remotely resemble that. It is as opposite as the poles. What does he do? Come together, the church assembles, they divide up the assembly into a plurality of classes, a plurality or staff of teachers they have, and they get all of them teaching at the same time, those respective groups. Paul shows that one teacher is to teach the church at a time, and if they have more to teach than one, they speak one at a time to all. The man doesn't know what a parallel is if he is trying to parallel that with his Sunday School. He'll never get out from under that. He cannot sustain it from any way. That is the predicament men get into when they fly off after the doctrines and commandments of men. (How much time, Brother Dennis? Three minutes? Six minutes. That's better. Thank you.)

I haven't been able to cover all of the notes which I took then, but now I shall drop back to the 14th chapter as I promised. Here the apostle says, "Let your women keep silence in the churches." Here the apostle says, "for it is not permitted unto them to speak, but they are commanded to be under obedience as also saith the law, and if they will learn anything let them ask their husbands at home, for it is a shame for a woman to speak in the church". The word, woman, there is defined to mean any woman, whether she is married, single, or a widow, according to the Lexicon. All right, the context shows that. (Thayer's Lexicon P. 123)

Now then, let's notice. (He is talking here to the prophets) "speak one by one", then he said to them, "Let your women keep silence in the churches." Wives of the prophets were not allowed to speak in the church. What is he talking about? Is the speaking here unlimited, Brother Porter said, or is it limited? I say that it is limited to the thing that he is talking about about in the context. Women are not allowed to address church assemblies. He knows that's what it's talking about. You just look at the eleven o'clock service where he preaches. Will he allow a woman, to teach there? No, it violates this. Will he allow her to speak in some other ways in that assembly? Yes, but he won't let her teach there per this, address the assembly. No. So you can see, my friends, that he knows its meaning and applies it like I do, in his eleven o'clock services. At the other services, or assemblies of the church, let no one think or try to believe that the church hadn't come together when they take the same people at eleven o'clock and teach them that they had at 10:30 or at some other time. It is the church of the Lord Jesus Christ, and he has taken that position in time past. It is an assembly of the church. "If they will learn anything let them ask their husbands at home". That is, if they would further investigate God's word they cannot do that in the assemblies of the church. The women are not allowed to do that, or seek for further information or ask questions, or to talk or to teach in that assembly. They cannot do that "for it is a shame for a woman to speak in the church." "If any man think himself to be a prophet or spiritual let him acknowledge that the things which I write unto you are the commandments of the Lord."

So then, tonight, dropping back we see this host of examples. Here we have Acts 20:7, just one example of them coming together to worship God and break bread and most of his brethren wouldn't divide the assembly to break bread for anything. They wouldn't do it in classes. The last debate I had, a man put up a big chart and said, "No, you can't divide up for the Lord's Supper in classes". What do they have to go by? *One example where they came together to break bread.* Why not, then, a host of examples showing they came together to be taught the word of God and they remained together and men only taught one by one and women learned in silence? And they got the job done and converted the world by the thousands. I defy any man to show a better method. If we could just get men and brethren to work in the Lord's appointed way there would be peace and unity and harmony and love, and souls would be saved for the Lord and Saviour, Jesus Christ. It is enough to make the hearts of all bleed that men will trample under foot and flagrantly set aside the commands of our Lord merely to exalt the doctrines and commandments of men and to follow the world in its mad rush to merely be popular, or something of that kind. It, my beloved, cannot surpass the Lord's plan in any way whatsoever. Oh, the Lord Jesus Christ has ordained that which will stand up. He is met with a veritable array of truth that he will never be able to recover from. He will, my friends, never be able to surmount the evidence which I have presented in this audience tonight, and I plead with you in the face of God and of high heaven to lay hold upon God's word. Don't take what I say or what he says, but take what God's word says after this discussion is over and you be governed by what the Bible says. We must all appear before the judgement seat of Christ that everyone may receive for the deeds done in his body according to that which he hath done, whether it be good or bad. This thing is going to confront Brother Porter and everyone else and all of us at the great judgement bar of God. Here is an array of scriptures that he will never be able to trample under foot or cause those who are seeking to know the truth not to understand them. They are too simple. My beloved, what did he say about "unbelievers"? "Saved and unsaved" and "Christians"? (on the chart)? Why, nothing. He couldn't do a thing with it. I showed here that they taught unbelievers, saved and unsaved and Christians in all their assemblies. Didn't have to segregate at all. They got the job done, they saved souls, they baptized thousands, they built up the church, they planted congregations. Can he do better? This is God's order, and we must recognize it and they that do not recognize it, God will not recognize them.

Porter's Second Speech
Dec. 4, 1951

Brethren, Moderators, Brother Abercrombie, Ladies and Gentlemen:

I appreciate another opportunity of replying to the speech which Cecil has just made. That, indeed, was a very fine exhortation that he used about the last five minutes of his time in telling you how people who used classes are adopting innovations and following after the doctrines and commandments of man, that we must all stand before the judgement bar of God and give an account for these things, and since we have all of these assemblies here on his chart, why then, of course, Porter is standing with the doctrines and commandments of men, and therefore will stand condemned after a while. But every word of that exhortation can be returned by the "one cup" brethren to Cecil. Everything that he says about the classes being an innovation, the doctrines and commandments of men, they turn right around and say the same thing to him about the plurality of cups. We notice that in everyone of these assemblies he gives that he cannot find the mention of the plurality of cups, and they come right back to him on the very same thing. What were these things written for, Cecil? Were they just to fill up space? Why, you find your plurality of cups in them somewhere. And all that exhortation that he gave to me can be turned right back on him by the "one cup" brethren. We stand or we fall together, Cecil. You must get on the side with us or you must get on the side with the "one cup" brethren. There is no way around it. You are occupying an inconsistent position that cannot be maintained.

Cecil, what was the matter with those questions I gave you?

Abercrombie speaking: "I'll answer them tomorrow night."

Porter: "You'll answer them tomorrow night? Well, I'll give you some more then to go with them. Well, now here we have it. We'll just have some more to go along with those since he waits until tomorrow night. I was hoping that he would get into them so we could actually get some of these things discussed without waiting too long in the debate. But he's

—35—

going to answer them tomorrow night. He, perhaps, can get some help sometime to get some answers for them, So he'll wait unto tomorrow night. Number Nine — (I'll hand this to you so that you can see it.)

9. Can two groups from the same congregation scripturally meet in separate places for simultaneous teaching and worship?

10. Does the command to sing ever include playing a mechanical instrument?

11. What percentage of the membership must assemble before it becomes a church assembly?

12. When the church comes together for the purpose of teaching, can a woman do any type of speaking or teaching in this assembly?

13. Can a sister scripturally call a group of sisters to her home and teach them?

14. Does the Bible authorize one teacher for one assembly?

15. Since a plurality of singers may sing at the same time without causing confusion, why cannot a plurality of speakers speak at the same time without causing such?

Well, we'll see if he gives us the answers to those tomorrow night, or if he just says on No. 5, "See No. 4;" and on No. 6 he'll say, "See No.5," and on No. 7 he'll say, "See No. 6," and on No. 8 he'll say, "See No. 7." That's the way he did in the other debate. I suppose that's the way he'll answer these. We'll wait and see.

Now, it is a fact that while anti-class brethren have had a great deal to say about teaching groups and classes, but nevertheless many of them are doing the very thing which they are condemning. There is a number of anti-class brethren over in the Kerrville, Texas section that publish the Gospel Tidings, which is an anti-class paper, and on the last page of this issue of the paper, August, 1951, they have a display ad. It has the large headline, saying, "THE FALL SESSION OF KEERVLLE BIBLE TRAINING WORK OPENS ON SEPTEMBER 10th. Make Your Plans Now To Attend.

The sixth long session (nine months) of the Kerrville Bible training work is scheduled to begin with the opening service at 7 p.m., Monday, September 10th, at the church building on Fredericksburg Road in Kerrville. Courses offered will include: Old Testament, New Testament, Vocal Music, Preparation and Delivery of Talks, Study of the Local Church, and Personal Work. Instructors are : J. D. Corder, Tomy Williams, and G. B. Shelburne, Jr."

Now, that is some anti-class brethren, believe it or not. And brethren are beginning to see through those things and many of their preachers who have been aligned with that very school work have given it up and taken their stand with us, because they have been able to see through that thing. Right while condemning classes and condemning the idea of teaching special groups, they are carrying on a school of nine month's duration in the year. Now, it has been running for some five or six years, in which they offer all these courses, which are simply Bible classes, along with vocal music and things of that kind. And besides, in the summer between the nine month's session, they have special sessions of the same work. Anti-Bible class brethren are doing that.

Cecil said, "Porter virtually acknowledged that the scriptures I have up here are the truth". No, he didn't, Cecil. "Porter virtually acknowledged the scriptures I have up here are the truth". *Porter always believed those scriptures were the truth.* I didn't *virtually acknowledge* any such thing. I take my stand tonight that *every scripture* he has on the board teaches the truth. I have *always contended* they teach the truth, but *I do not acknowledge the law which Cecil reads into them.* That's the point. I do not acknowledge that his application of those scriptures is the truth. I don't deny the scriptures. He has just made a misapplication of them, that's all. But he said, "He just acknowledged that", and then I "quibbled" about a lot of other things. And he says when we differ on something else, then we'll debate that.

If we differ on the radio, we'll have a debate about the radio; and if we differ about singing schools, we'll have a debate about that. Said it might be a sin to preach on the radio, and it might not, but that's not the issue. Now "when Porter believes that it is a sin, when he takes the position that it is sin, then I'm willing to debate him on it, but until we do, why that's not the issue". Yes. Yes, when we differ about those things. "That's not the issue." But what's the trouble? Cecil is not willing for his practice to be brought before an audience and let them look at it and see his inconsistency. That's what I'm showing. I'm showing that a man who has enough intelligence to see that the command to teach would include

—37—

preaching on the radio or teaching a singing school ought to be able to see that it includes other methods of teaching, too. That's the point. Certainly so, but we'll have more about that just a little bit later as we come to the notes.

"Porter believes the one cuppers are just as wrong as I do." Yes, and I believe that you are just as wrong as they are when it comes to this matter tonight. Yes, I believe that you are just as wrong as they are. They're making a law where God has not made it when they say that you must have one drinking vessel, and Cecil's making a law where God hasn't made it when he says the assembly must remain one group. There is just not any verse that says either of them. One is just as wrong as the other.

About this word, "should". He said, "Now, Porter wanted to know if that would send people to hell. He's trying to get a little prejudice". Oh, no, I do not need any prejudice to meet you fellows. No at all. I am just trying to get your idea about it. Just want to see what you believe about it, that's all. Just how strong you believe the word "must" is. That's all. I'm not trying to create any prejudice. I don't need any. I can take care of many of them like you, Cecil, and not have to use any prejudice at all. They'll have to try out something they haven't yet tried out. I'll have to see something that I've never seen in order to make me fear any anti-Bible class advocate beneath the stars.

But he said this about this "must", "Now, I'll just ask him, "Must" those teachers speak as Paul said?" Yes, sir, Cecil, when they are speaking *to one assembly* they *must* do it; one teacher to one assembly, one teacher to one group. Certainly so. That's all the Lord said. But when you read into it, *they "must" remain* in one assembly, Paul didn't say that, Cecil. Did you read it anywhere in 1 Cor. 14? If you'll show it to me, I'll read it to the audience. *Will you show me where Paul said that in 1 Cor. 14?* Let me read it to the audience. I can read it to the audience. Where Paul said, "They must remain in one assembly". Now, while they're in one assembly, as long as that one assembly stays there, certainly those speakers must teach as Paul said they must. One speaker to one group, Cecil. But Paul never said *they must remain in one group;* and that's where you're putting a law that God never did give. On, he said Paul used that "must". No, Paul didn't. Paul didn't either.

By the way, Cecil, I wish I knew about this. I wish I knew right now. Does that teaching program in your proposition cover this assembly tonight? Huh? Would you answer that for us tomorrow night, Cecil? Does your proposition cover the assembly in this building tonight? If so, Cecil's going to hell, because they are not all in one group. Some of them are here, some of them are out yonder, and some of them are in the basement, and all around in different places, and different rooms, and Cecil's teaching them. And yet he says the law says that *they must remain on one group.* They must remain in one assembly. Cecil's gone to hell on his own proposition. That's the inconsistency of anti-class hobbyists.

But "the denominations came along with the Sunday School, and it went right into the church over our protests like every other innovation," he says. And when the denominations came along with their plurality of cups in the communion service, they went right into the church of Christ with Cecil and his group over the protests of the other brethren. Now, don't you see the parallel? He says there's not any parallel along that line. You see the Parallels. There has been no more protests against the classes by Cecil and those who stand with him than there has been among the other brethren against Cecil's plurality of cups. *Not a bit.* No, sir. He said, "Why, they said we want them; we're going to have them. We don't care what the book of God says; we're going to have them anyway". And other say, "Well, Cecil says we don't care what the book of God says. It said Jesus took *the cup,* and every place where you find it mentioned, it's mentioned in the singular number. But Cecil does not care what the book of God says. We want the plurality of cups; the denominations have them; we want them just like them. So we're going to bring them in over your protests." And so the division resulted. What's sauce for the goose is sauce for the gander.

By the way, Cecil, I'm just wondering *if the missionary society is an issue tonight?* You know how Cecil talked about all that when I brought up the cups, and the radio preaching and the singing schools. He said, "Now, when we differ on that, we'll debate on it, but until we differ on that, then that's not the issue". Well, Cecil, when we differ about the missionary society, we'll debate on that. As long as we don't differ on it, then, according to your position, you have no right to bring it in. Why did you bring it in, Cecil? Do we differ on it?

Is that the issue? You brought it in, didn't you, Cecil? Yes, Cecil brought it in. But that's not the issue. *We don't even differ on it.* He'll admit that we don't even differ on that, but he tries to make a parallel. Now, he thinks that he has a perfect right to make a parallel of the Missionary Society and the Sunday School, but Porter has no right to make a parallel of the cups and the class teaching and the radio preaching and the singing school. Porter doesn't have any right to make any parallels. *That right belongs exclusively to Cecil Abercrombie.* The Lord has given him a special permit along that line. So he can just bring it in, but Porter has no right to do it. Don't you see?

Regarding 1 Cor. 14:31, he said, "Cecil made no law. Porter charges that Cecil made a law." But he said, "Cecil made no law." 1 Cor. 14:31: "For ye may all prophesy one by one, that all may learn, and all may be comforted", and in verse 37 Paul said that "these things that I write are the commandments of the Lord." He said Paul make that law — that Cecil didn't make it. "Porter said Cecil wrote that." No, Porter didn't. No, Porter didn't say Cecil wrote that. Porter said Cecil *read into it something that Paul didn't say,* and I'm still standing on it. Certainly, that's what Paul said, but Cecil read into it something that Paul didn't say. Now, Paul said, "Ye may all prophesy one by one" to one assembly, and, furthermore, he said, "I am writing the commandments of the Lord." *But Paul did not say that you must remain in an undivided assembly.* Paul didn't say that. That's the law that Cecil made. I know Paul made these laws here, but Cecil added one to it that Paul didn't state. That's the point I made. You missed it completely. Cecil, I think that you know what I didn't say that you wrote 1st Cor. 14:31 and 37. I know that this audience knows that I didn't say that you wrote that, but I said you read into it something that it didn't say: *that they must remain in one group,* that *they must remain in an undivided assembly.* Paul didn't say that. The word of God doesn't say that. I challenge you Cecil, every inch of you from the top of your head to the soles of your feet to give me the verse that says it. You didn't. Tomorrow night, Cecil? We'll wait and see.

"Porter argues that there is no 'how' given, there's no method: so if there's no way or no method given, then," he said, "Paul wasted the whole chapter, and this chapter doesn't mean anything to Porter." Yes, it does. And the chapter is not wasted, because Paul is regulating the teaching in *one particular group*. But Paul gave no regulations that they must remain in one group. That's *your regulation*, Cecil, and it is not in Paul's writing at all. You can't find it in any assembly in any scripture you have on the board. It just isn't there. If it is, when he comes to the platform tomorrow night I want him to underscore the passage that says that — the passage that says, "You must remain in an undivided assembly." Let him underscore the passage that says that. When he does I'll just shake hands with him and close the debate, and say it's over, Cecil, I'll go right along with you. I'm not uneasy. Don't get scared. But Paul declared that all are to learn from all the teachers in the assembly. I never disputed that that all are to learn from all of the teachers in the assembly.

But he said, "Now, Paul couldn't have preached over the radio if he had wanted to, but he could have used the classes." Well, then the classes are older than the radio, aren't they? He talks about classes being a modern innovation. Well, the classes are older than the radio, then according to his own argument, for he says, "Paul couldn't have used the radio, but he could have used the classes." So he admits that the classes are older than the radio. If he is going to operate upon the basis, from the standpoint, of which is the most modern, then he'll have to give up his radio preaching, because it is more modern than the classes, according to his own argument, according to his own statement.

He wanted to know, then, how in the world can you stretch Matt. 28:19 to include the classes, but to exclude the Missionary Societies? I stretch it, Cecil, exactly the same way that you stretch it to include the Singing School but to exclude the Missionary Societies. Now, you tell me how you can stretch Matt. 28:19 to include the Singing School, as taught by you brethren, and at the same time exclude the Missionary Society. When you tell me how you can stretch that, I stretch it the same way. *Come on, now, and tell us tomorrow night.*

Regarding Acts 2, I said he skipped down to verse 14, but he said, "Porter skipped to verse 5. What did you skip for?" Well, I didn't skip. You had already read that. I just started where you quit reading, Cecil. You had already read those verses, and I just took up where you made the skip. That was all. I wasn't skipping anything that hadn't already been read to the audience, and I just started where you stopped. That was the point. I didn't skip. I merely started where you stopped.

Now, we're going back to Acts 2, and see a little more about that. Acts": "When the day of Pentecost was fully come, they were all with one accord in one place, and suddenly there came from heaven the sound as of a rushing mighty wind, and it filled all the house where they were sitting. And there appeared unto them cloven tongues like as of fire, and it sat upon each of them. And they were all filled with the Holy Ghost, and began to speak with other tongues as the Spirit gave them utterance. And there were dwelling at Jerusalem Jews, devout men, out of every nation under heaven". Now, that's the five verses that he read, and then I took over where he stopped. "Now, when this was noised abroad, the multitude came together, and were confounded, because that every man heard them speak in his own language", and Cecil wanted to Know — let me see. (Looks at notes). Yes, Cecil wanted to know, Since the multitude can together after they began to speak with other tongues as the spirit gave them utterance, who were they teaching in the first place? Well, the same group they were teaching according to your position. Whom, do you say they were teaching in the first place when the multitude came together? Huh? If that means anything against me, it means the same thing against you, Cecil. I didn't say they were teaching before the multitude came together, but the passage I read was after the multitude came together. After the multitude came together, then the multitude said, "Are not all these which speak (or which *are speaking,* as some translations give it) Galileans?" "Are not all these which are speaking Galileans? And how hear we every man in our own tongue, wherein we were born?" Those statements were made, Cecil, *after the multitude came together:* not before it came together, but after it came together. And he said Porter had twelve men all talking at one place at the same time. Well, the multitude hadn't even come together in that passage you endeavor to base your argument on. That's before the multitude came together. That doesn't help you in the least. But he said that all spoke just like Peter did in verse 14. All the others were silent. Peter therefore spoke in all of the languages, and the rest of them kept still. He addressed the

—42—

whole audience in all the different languages, and they all understood, and Peter delivered about (he said) seventeen different sermons on that occasion in seventeen different languages. He said seventeen languages, or something like that, and then he qualified that. In the other debate he said *seventeen languages,* and I called his attention to the fact that there were not seventeen. and he said, "Well, I assumed there were". He has done a lot of assuming, but he hasn't proven yet.

1 Cor. 14 says that tongue speakers must speak one at a time, and these were tongue speakers. Yes, 1 Cor. 14 says tongue speakers must speak one at a time before one assembly, before one group, but Cecil said, "There was no division here. They were divided according to language, Porter says, but," he says, "that does not fit your class. You don't divide them according to language. That doesn't fit your class." Well, do you speak in various languages to you assembly? *Does it fit yours?* No, he doesn't speak in various languages to one assembly. It doesn't fit his then, according to that. But *they were divided according to language,* and said, "How *hear we* every man in our own tongue, wherein we were born." But "there were a plurality of speakers, and all together, and they all remained together," he said, "and Porter has the idea that the murderers, those murderers, would be so calm as to allow the apostles to classify and segregate them and teach them and them bring them back in, give them further explanation in Peter's sermon." Peter didn't classify them according to languages. They were already classified according to languages. *That classification existed already.* They already spoke various languages in which they were born. That classification existed already, and each man was addressed in his own language, in his own tongue. They merely recognized that the classification already existed by virtue of the language situation.

"Porter charged unjustly that I want the details." He said, "In some things the details are not given; therefore, I don't want them." No, you don't want them where it concerns your practice, but you want them where it concerns the other fellow's practice. That's what I was talking about. I didn't say Cecil wanted the details for everything. That is the very thing I said that he didn't want. For everything that he does, he doesn't want any details; but for the other man, he wants all the details given, you see. That's the point I made. Cecil missed it completely. He wants all the details for Bible class work, but he can get along without the details when it comes to radio preaching. He can get along without the details when it come to teaching a singing school. He can get along without the details when it come to taking up the collection in a basket, or a box, or what have you? He can get along without details when it come to the number of vessels you can use in the communion service. On all those things he can get along without the details. He doesn't want details regarding a debate. He doesn't have to have the proof that Paul challenged Peter for a debate; in the second place, that they signed propositions; in the third place, they alternated speaking every thirty minutes; and the fourth place, James and John moderated for them. He didn't want that; he doesn't have to have details for that. He's doing that. But for the class teaching he must have all the details, or it's unscriptural. That's what I said, and if you're going to demand that the class teacher furnish details for every little matter, then, to be consistent, you must furnish them for your own practice, He doesn't want his practice held up before the audience. He wants you to forget about that, but I am determined that whenever I meet Cecil in a debate the audience is going to know about his practice. He's not going to keep it in the background. I'm going to see that they know about it.

He comes to 1 Cor. 14:31 "Porter", he says, "applies this to the classes — 'All may learn and all may be comforted.' Therefore, he must rotate his teachers to every class so that they may hear all the teachers in the assembly, and that puts the women teaching men." So he must rotate all the teachers to all the groups. No, 1 Cor. 14:31 concerns one group. It gives a law regarding the teachers for one group, Cecil, not for more than one group, but for one group, and where teachers are teaching one group, then they speak one at a time. *We have never violated that principle.* In our class teaching we never have but one teacher speaking to one group at a time. *It never occurs in our class teaching.* I no more hold to that idea than I would any other idea contrary to the book of God. But we don't have to rotate the teachers. All *in that group can hear everyone that might teach in that group,* and all in some other group can hear all that might teach in that group. Paul's regulation concerned only the teachers for that particular group, that particular assembly.

Then he turned right around and said, "but Porter wouldn't let a woman teach a man." Cecil, do you actually believe that? Cecil, did you ever hear me say that a woman couldn't teach a man? Huh? You remember, Cecil, in our debate up in Tennessee last year, you made that same charge in that written negative that you had (wrote it out and had it completed before the affirmative was ever delivered), and in that written negative, you said that *Porter will not allow a woman to teach a man.* I came back in my next speech and told you, "Don't you ever misrepresent me that way again; don't come up and say any more that Porter will not let a woman teach a man". Porter has never said any such thing. And yet in your very next speech you came back and made the same statement. After all that's been done, then you come down here in this debate and say Porter will not allow a woman to teach a man. Porter never made a statement like that in his life, Cecil, and you never heard him make a statement like that. *Did you?* Come on, now, tell me. Shake or nod, yes or no. *Did you ever hear me say that? Come on,* Cecil, Do tell me. Won't you tell the audience?

Moderator, Brother Dennis, speaking: "He'll answer you tomorrow night."

Porter: "Then will he, sure enough?"

Brother Dennis: "You know he will. Just talk to the audience."

Porter: "That's all right. I'm running-"

Brother Dennis: "You're out of order."

Porter: "I am not out of order. I can ask him a question when I want to, and you just keep your seat, and I'll attend to my business."

Brother Dennis: "I'll not keep my seat either."

Porter: "All right. You just go ahead. I'm attending to this. I'll make my own speech, and he'll make his. And if you are afraid for him to answer, why, that's all right. I don't care. He made the charge. He made the charge that Porter will not allow a woman to teach a man, and this audience has a right to know whether he ever heard Porter say that or not, and perhaps there are many in this audience who will not be here tomorrow night, and they'll never know what he says tomorrow night. Therefore, I insist he ought to shake or nod now and tell me whether he ever heard me make a statement like that. Did you, Cecil? *Come, on.* I know it hurts. *I know it hurts, but come on.* It's going to hurt more as we go along.

1 Cor. 14:34-35 again — "The woman," he say, "means any woman". The wives of the prophets were not allowed to speak, and speaking," he says, "is limited." Yes, sir, he said, "I'll admit that speaking is limited." Let's shake hands on that, Cecil. Let's shake hands on that — that teaching and speaking in 1 Cor. 14 is not unlimited. You said it. Well, you agree with me. Will you shake hands with me if that's so — that the speaking and teaching of 1 Cor. 14 is not unlimited? But Cecil reserves the right to put the limit on it and says Porter has no right to make any limitation. Let Cecil do it, you see. He's the one to do the limiting; Porter doesn't have any right. So speaking *is limited,* he said, to speaking in what it talks about there, and she is not allowed to speak in the eleven o'clock service, or in any service of the church, and she cannot seek any information in other church assemblies. Well, I'll just pass that by for the time being and let him give us some more about it tomorrow night. We want to see those questions answered.

His final part was on Acts 20:7. How much time do I have? About two or three minutes? "Two minutes." Moderator Dillingham speaks.

All right, The 20th chapter of Acts, verse 7, "And upon the first day of the week, when the diciples came together to break bread, Paul preached unto them, and continued his speech until midnight." And here, he says, "We have *one example* where they came together to break bread, and they didn't divide into classes to break bread. But he says we have a whole host of examples where they came together for teaching. And Porter will say that they can't break bread in the classes, but they can teach in the classes." Well, we'll just turn that around in this one example and the other examples given in the book of God. Do you have anything said about the plurality of cups in the communion service? Huh? I know Cecil doesn't like to hear that. I wouldn't either if I were in his position. Huh? I'd be sick of it, too. But he's going to get so sick he may want the doctor before we get through with this thing. Yes, sir. Cecil's sick of the cup business, but he's going to hear it, and it's going to keep on ringing in his ears, because he's occupying an inconsistent position. The "one cup" brethren say that in all of these assemblies there is never any mention made of anything except "the" cup - "the cup, the cup, this cup, that cup, a cup, the cup". You've heard it, haven't you, Cecil? We've both debated them, haven't we? And you've always heard them say "the cup, a cup, this cup, that cup," haven't you? And it's always cup in the singular number,isn't it? Always cup in the singular number. All right, then he turns right around and says that we can have cups in the plural number. In any of these assemblies he cannot find his plurality of cups. So I insist that he must either be turned over to the "one cup" brethren — give up his contention here on this matter, and take up with the "one cup" brethren, or he must come to us. He can't occupy a position between us. The "one cup" brethren are far more consistent than Cecil is, I'll say that for them. If any of them are in the audience tonight, I'll just say that you "one cup" brethren, if you're here tonight, you who believe in *one literal container,* you occupy a far more consistent position than Cecil occupies. Much more, for he makes the same argument in favor of his cups that he condemns me for making respect to class teaching. He makes it on one hand, and he condemns it on the other. Didn't Paul say something about that man, "Happy is the man that condemneth not himself in that thing which he allows"? And that's exactly where Cecil stands. He condemns himself with the very principle with which he tries to condemn somebody else. Thank you, Ladies and Gentlemen.

Abercrombie's First Speech
Second Night — December 5, 1951

Fellow Moderators, Ladies and Gentlemen, Worthy Opponent:

It is with great pleasure I stand before you this afternoon to affirm the proposition, "The scriptures teach that to teach the church assembled we are to remain in one assembly, and be taught by men only speaking one at a time." I think Brother Dennis made just a slight error in the reading of it, and I didn't give it exactly, but that's the gist of it.

We are here to set forth what the scriptures teach. We proved by the precious word of God last evening that which the Lord will receive and accept in divine service. We have set forth from the scriptures the divine plan of teaching, God's good order of eliminating confusion and edifying the church. This we find holds good in all assemblies, 1 Cor. 14:33, "As in all assemblies (or churches) of the saints." This the apostle has commanded in verse 37, and we find that these issues are before us. 1 Cor. 14:40, "Let all things be done decently and in order". I set forth from Matt. 18:20, Heb. 20:25, Jas. 2:2, scriptures showing that the church came together, authority for the church to assemble. In Acts 2nd chapter, verse 6, Acts 11:26, Acts 20:7-8, Acts 14:27-28, and Acts 15:25-33 — from these scriptures we gave examples of the church assembling, or of the apostles, who were inspired men, preaching the word of God, and in none of these did we find division into classes. On the other side of the chart, in Acts 2 we find that one teacher taught the multitude that came together, and no division into classes or segregating of the assembly for the purpose of teaching the word of God. In the Third Chapter we find the apostle Peter doing the preaching, and no division into classes.

My friends and brethren, if this thing was as important as some of my brethren contend and that my opponent contends, it seems that somewhere in the word of God they wouldn't have omitted it entirely. They would have hinted at it, they would have put it in there or told us something about it. Certainly if it is as important as they contend, we would have an outline or detail showing how to group and grade or classify the church. But it isn't there. They had a better method than that, and that is found in 1 Cor. 14:31 where the apostle Paul commanded, "Ye may all prophesy one by one that all may learn and all may be comforted". Thus we have set forth from the scriptures, this, that positively forbids the grouping and grading of the people when the church assembles to be taught. God's order is that men should do the teaching. Verse 35 says, "It is a shame for women to speak in the church", and so we find that these restrictions are levied upon the assemblies of the saints when they convene to teach the word of the Lord and Saviour, Jesus Christ. These things we wholeheartedly endorse and strive diligently to obey and exhort men and women everywhere to comply with. It is indeed difficult to get very many people today to obey the gospel of the Son of God as it is written. We find that my opponent has argued and insisted that he practices this by the class system, but friends, they are as diametrically opposed as anything can be. There the apostle says to the teachers (and they were men) to speak one by one that all may learn. All would learn from all of the teachers and all be comforted. They would be comforted from all the teachers, thus showing that they remained together and men only did the teaching and they spake one by one unto all. Thus we have proven our practice. This we follow, this is according to the word of God.

Acts, 2nd chapter, we find when unbelievers were taught they did not segregate them into classes and have a plurality of teachers with some women teachers as my opponent affirms can be done, and as he practices. It cannot be found in the word of God. Here we find they did not segregate to teach the word of God. 1 Cor. 14:23-25, the church assembled, and we find that saved and unsaved came together. They did not segregate to teach the word of God. Even tongue speakers were not allowed to go into classes and exercise their gift, in the absence of an interpreter. If they had no interpreter he couldn't speak in the assembly. And so we find that God's order kept them in one place, one assembly when the church convened.

Now then we turn to Acts 20:7, showing where Christians assembled. They did not divide into classes for the teaching. In the 1 Cor. letter we mentioned the tongue speakers. Now we take up verse 31 again, "For ye may all prophesy one by one that all may learn and all may be comforted". This, when it is followed today, will do away with the grouping and grading and classifying of the assembly because we see that God's plan is superior to the wisdom of man. No man can devise any scheme of teaching that will out-class that which the God of

Heaven devised for the ancient assemblies of the church of Jesus Christ. I am earnestly contending for the truth that was once delivered unto the saints, and I hope and trust that you will weigh these scriptures well and take them for what they're worth and be obedient unto the same.

In verse 34-35, "Let your women keep silence in the churches, for it is not permitted unto them to speak, but they are commanded to be under obedience as also saith the law, and if they will learn anything let them ask their husbands at home, for it is a shame for a woman to speak in the church". The wives of the prophets were silenced and the general underlying principle that silenced them was — "It is a shame for women to speak in the church." The limitation there is on the thing the apostle was speaking about concerning teaching or addressing, teaching the church. That is forbidden by the word of the Lord Jesus Christ. Now then, that is what we practice. That is what we follow and I have sustained our practice and my proposition.

Now then I shall take up just a few things that took place here last evening. You remember that just before the closing speech, before Brother Porter ended his talk, he tried to have a lots of sport. He tried to deal in things that are unbecoming a discussion of this kind, and such things as that. He inferred that I had misrepresented him in saying that Brother Porter forbids women to teach men. Now, from the beginning of this discussion I have affirmed that we are discussing what the church should do when it assembles and the class system of teaching, and I trust, I thought that was amply clear throughout this discussion, that Brother Porter did not believe that women could teach men in Sunday School classes. That has been his position for the last three discussions that I know of, and if he has changed I didn't know it, and if he has changed on that, I just didn't know that and I beg his pardon. And so he will probably have more to say about that and let us know, but he knew what I was talking about and got over here in my face and tried to have a lot of fun and make it appear that I had misrepresented him. "Did you ever hear me say that women could not teach men?" Why, I've heard him say it many times, that they couldn't teach men in his classes. Furthermore, in his last debate at Quincy, Ill., I think it is, the third session and second negative, Brother Porter, in reference to preaching over the radio, he said that a sister, if there were

—50—

only women listening in, "I would say, yes, she could teach or preach or teach over the radio if only women were listening in." Let him deny that. Third session and second negative with reference to preaching over the radio, he said that women could preach over the radio if there were only women listening in, "I would say, yes." Then he got over here and asked me those questions, "Now, did you ever hear me say that women couldn't teach men?" What other conclusion could I come to?

Now then, he presented several questions, about fourteen in number. In my last discussion I received 54 typewritten questions by my opponent to be answered by me in the last speech of the debate, or the last session rather, and it took my opponent, Brother Gus Nichols, part of both of his speeches just to read them. That shows you some of the tricks in putting out a whole lot of questions that usually are merely technicalities that do not apply to his practice and what he is doing, whatsoever, but we will oblige him with answers. He won't like them. No sir. I don't expect him to like them. He may say they weren't answered. They generally do.

1. What characteristics must an assembly possess in order to constitute a church assembly?

Answer: I accept you definition given in your debate with Brother Waters at Quincy, which was Matthew 18:20.

2. Is a Bible class or a Sunday School class a church assembly?

Answer: Since you said last night 1 Cor. 14:31 applied to classes in Sunday School you defined it as a church assembly.

3. Is it a sin to divide the church assembly?

Answer: When the church assembles for the purpose of teaching it is sinful to divide into Sunday School classes. This is the issue of our proposition.

4. How far must some be removed from others before the assembly becomes divided?

Answer: Some Sunday School churches divide into classes in the same room. Others more able financially build rooms to the main auditorium. All such divisions are sinful. This is the issue of this discussion.

5. Are two things ever parallel in one point but not parallel in another?

Answer: Sunday School is parallel with the Missionary Society in claiming Matt. 28:19 as proof, and they are parallel in both being the doctrines that commandments of men, but they are not parallel in that the Sunday School does not send missionaries to foreign lands.

6. Can two men scripturally preach from two radio stations operating on different killocycles in separate rooms of the same building at the same time?

Answer: If you mean this to be a parallel with the Sunday School class, may a woman speak over one of these radio stations? Yes, they can if the men will just turn off and the women would tune in (Quincy Debate — Porter's Doctrine).

7. Can the church scripturally call together a special group for special training?

Answer: If you mean by training 1 Cor. 14 regulates teaching in church assemblies. If you mean Sunday School as we are debating, no.

8. Can two groups from two different congregations scripturally meet in separate places for simultaneous teaching and worship?

Answer: If you mean that these two groups are starting a new congregation, then 1 Cor. 14 regulates it. If you mean Sunday School classes as practiced by you and your brethren, no.

9. That's the same as No. 8. He said, "See that other". That's the same, you look on your notes. That's the same question.

10. Does the command (that was just a duplicate question) Does the command to sing ever include playing a mechanical insturment?

Answer: A musical instrument is found in sing just like you find divide into classes in the command to teach. Both are added by men and sinful.

11. What percentage of the membership must assemble before it becomes a church assembly?

Answer: I accept the teaching of Matt. 18:20 on this and your teaching on this scripture.

12. When the church comes together for the purpose of teaching, can a woman do any type of speaking or teaching in this assembly?

Answer: Women may engage in congregational singing per Col. 3:16.

13. Can a sister scripturally call a group of sisters to her

home and teach them?

Answer: Women can teach according to Acts 21:9. She can teach a man according to Act 18:26. Aged women can teach young women according to Titus 2:3-5. Not in church assemblies, though. Now let's enlarge on Brother Porter's group in the question. If 150 or all of the women in town responded to her call, *this is a called meeting of this woman*, and her husband and five grown boys at home; she calls on them for help in arranging seating room and to build fires and to keep them going while her called meeting was going on. Fifteen out of this group are convinced that Jesus Christ is the Son of God and they decide to obey her teaching and confess Christ and be baptized, and then two of her unbelieving boys and her unbelieving husband become believers and desire baptism. This excites the sister and she runs to the phone and calls the preacher, the only male member of the congregation, and lo! and behold! He won't be back for six days. Must she refuse to take their confession and baptise them? Remember Brother Porter, this is a called meeting of this sister, a called group. What about that all women Church of Christ at Montevallo, Alabama, with a sister in charge, just six miles from another Church of Christ, and it was started by the "green light" of Brother John T. Lewis? All women Church of Christ! That's what they're going to. They're running to that. They're going to soon be consistent! Just about six miles from Montevallo, there's another Church of Christ that has men. All right. Brother J. L. Hines says in Gospel Broadcast, March 25, 1943, "Look in Matt, 28:19. Use a little reasoning and you will find a woman in there baptizing". Find a woman that can baptise Matthew. It is wonderful what these boys can dig out of Matt. 28:19, "If you'll just use a little reasoning". Find a woman there baptizing! All right. If he can draw up cases, we can too.

14. Does the Bible authorize one teacher for one assembly?

Answer: God authorized one teaching at a time to an assembly of the church, 1 Cor. 14:31, or according to, my proposition.

15. Since a plurality of singers may sing at the same time without causing confusion, why cannot a plurality of speakers speak at the same time without causing such?

Answer: We are commanded to sing, Eph. 5:19, in the assembly. Col. 3 shows all are to sing. Paul says for the teachers to speak one by one that all may learn and all may be comforted. That's the difference.

That compliments the questions as propounded by Brother Porter in this discussion, and so we shall proceed with more pertinent things to this discussion.

My proposition say, "The Scriptures Teach". I'm going to do a little reading. Brother Porter likes to hear me read! I have tried to get Brother Porter to stay with the issue, but he refuses. He wants to get your minds confused by injecting seven or eight or ten more issues not the subject of this debate. We are contending that where God has given details they must be followed. Porter knows that teach is restricted by way of example and command, and we have forced him to abandon the false position which he usually takes on Matt. 28:19, for he now applies 1 Cor. 14:31 to church assemblies. Yes, even to the church assembly for class teaching. *If this command is followed it will not allow classes.* Paul is regulating the human voice in teaching services of all assemblies of the saints where the word of God is taught. *Now, since Porter applies 1 Cor. 14:31 to the church assembly for class teaching, he must also carry 1 Cor. 14:35 "For it is a shame for women to speak in the church". With verse 31, so it knocks his women entirely out of the Sunday School. Verse 35 applies where verse 31 applies, and Porter applies both to his eleven a.m. meeting on Lord's Day.* If the brethren here follow Brother Porter's teaching they will have to stop women teaching in the church assembly for Sunday Schools, and that will just about kill the whole thing. It is just an invention to put women teaching in church assemblies.

At Taft, Tennessee, Porter drew this distinction between the Missionary Society and the Sunday School. *The Missionary Society is a separate organization. The Sunday School assembly is the church.* It is the church organized into a Sunday School, I tried to get Porter to stay with the issue set forth in my proposition, but he would not and insisted that I take up matters in my affirmative. It would have been better for Porter's lost cause if he had not gone all over the country trying to find junk to clutter up this debate.

I have proven my practice by the word of God, so now we shall accommadate him on a few other things that he wants me to discuss. I'll notice a few of his quibbles. He said last night that I said they had classes and that therefore the radio was younger than classes". Here is what I said. "The *apostle could have had classes*, but rejected them, but they could not have preached over a radio because it had not been discovered." The record will show this. That is what I said almost word for word. Porter is notorious for twisting words. He shall not get by with it.

Singing Schools — God has not told us how to teach the science of music, but he has told us how to teach his word in the assemblies of the saints. We have congregational singing lead by a man. We sing together. This is in harmony with the scriptures. He practices that and I practice that. That is in harmony with the word of God. At Taft, Tennessee, Brother Porter said that there wasn't a singing school in the Bible, and that where I found a singing school in the Bible he would find his Sunday School. The Bible would include the Old Testament. I stated that I didn't rely on the Old Testament for proof for my practice, didn't offer it for that, but I invited all to listen to 1 Chron. 25:6-7 to show that Porter didn't know what he was talking about. I quoted or read that and didn't give the quotation. He said, "Where is that?", and I said, "I don't believe I'll even tell him", and then in a little while he got up and said, "Why, I knew it was in the Bible all the time", and had been affirming that it wasn't in the Bible, and I showed that they had song instruction there. He was going to find a Sunday School in that same place where I found song instruction in the Bible. I found that many there were instructed in the songs of the Lord and Lo! Porter said there would be his Sunday School and it had musical instruments in it, too. Sunday School and musical instruments go together. If I could swallow the Sunday School I could take the musical instrument without a dose of water after it. *They're both additions.* They're the doctrines and commandments of men. He wants me to discuss such things as this.

Now then, we'll talk a little about organized Sunday Schools and superintendents. We now shall notice the organization of the Sunday School. In the Firm Foundation literature for Sunday School they have it grouped up this way: Primary Dept. - Age 4 to 6; Junior Dept. - Age 7 to 15; Young People's and Adult Dept. - 16 to 18 years old; and of course there are various other departments in this organization. Now then, that is what they are practicing all over the country. It's organized into *departments. Departments of what? The*

Sunday School departments. Organized. All right, what are they doing? Why, they are issuing diplomas. Yes, diplomas. They graduate, you know in this thing, and certificates of promotion, and in the last edition of the Gospel Advocate book on Sunday School supplies they're giving little rewards and badges. Church of Christ Sunday School on them. You can get those for about fifty or sixty cents a piece. Now then, what about Sunday School superintendents? Why do they fight Superintendents of Sunday School? Well, they know that that's an office not known in the Bible and that makes it look like a separate organization, something organized, something different from the church. All right, do they believe in superintendents? We're going to notice some things in connection with that. This debate was advertised in Brother George Henry Peter Showalter's paper, "Firm Foundation". George Henry Peter has a Sunday School superintendent in the church where he worships. Gospel Advocate, they have Sunday School superintendents, and so, friends, we're going to now give him some of the stuff that he wants.

First we shall notice, here is a certificate issued by the Church of Christ, 12th Avenue, in Nashville, Tennessee, G. S. Dunn, superintendent, and was issued to Brother J. M. Sherril, certificate of attendance for School's Cross and Crown. Over here is a picture of Robert Raikes, founder of Sunday Schools, 1780, and over here is a picture of his first Sunday School. I want you to see it if you don't believe it. That's a photostatic copy. Brother Van Bonneau, I think, has the orginal. That's it. And they don't believe in it! I have also this I picked up from the Gospel Advocate. Here's the "Record for Sunday School." Now then, we notice over here on the first page, "Roll of Officers and Teachers" and so and so. Here are the officers. Did you ever read of any of these officers in the Bible? "Superintendents, Assistant Superintendents, the Secretary, the Treasurer, the Librarian, and the Teachers." There is the set-up of your organization. Well, so much for that.

Now then, here we find Sunday School literature published by the Gospel Advocate, on the back of this is a book they advertise, "Four Minute Talks for Superintendents". That's the superintendents of the Church of Christ Sunday School. Now then, we can offer much more. Here we have two catalogs and they are just full of Sunday School supplies for superintendents, and we can offer much more in proof of this thing.

At Lawrenceburg, Tennessee, Brother Porter claimed not to believe in superintendents prior to our debate in Taft, Tennessee. Yet the church he was called to defend advertised two superintendents of Sunday School. *Then he tried to defend them.* He made the same claim at Taft, and then when reminded of these things, and when reminded that they had a superintendent at Taft he then tried to defend such. Compared them like appointing a janitor. They don't want people to know that they have that added officer. "Cecil's trying to cover up what he's doing." Look at that man! They don't want the people to know what they've got. He condemns all the Baptists' and Methodists' Sunday Schools, they're all unscriptural. But he's got one that's essentially the same in build-up and it is all right. Classes, plurality of teachers, men and women teaching, and so on. Essentially it is the same. The doctrine taught might be a little different. All right, they don't want people to know they have that added officer to look after an organization unknown to the word of God.

The Gospel Advocate now offers medals, pins to wear for faithful Sunday School attendance, and on them is "Church of Christ". Now, "consistency", I want to show you how the Sunday School preachers have reached consistency! Brother Porter brought in last night Brother Shelburne's paper and report of his work in Texas. He said a lot of his brethren (my brethren) are getting their eyes open, they are seeing through this thing; that is, they are leaving us. They never do tell you about how many are leaving them a coming over to us. My knowledge of that work out there is that it's public, it's open and the preaching is done by one man teaching at a time just like we're doing here in this open public assembly. That's Porter grabbing at a straw. He's a drowning man. Sunday School preachers hardly ever tell about those who leave them. Now then, he says that they're getting their eyes open. Yes, and a lot of his brethren are getting their eyes open to the truth and leaving them.

Take a look now at this. Here's something. I want to show you some consistency! "God's Woman", my friends, there's a book that says, "To apply 1 Cor. 14 today is to pervert the word of God." Yes, to pervert the word of God, and a host of these Sunday School preachers endorse it, the Gospel

—57—

Advocate endorses it, and Firm Foundation endorses it. Brother Nichols said, "It's worth its weight in gold". Horace W. Busby endorses it. T. H. Etheridge, C. E. Woodridge, Cled E. Wallace, G. H. P. Showalter, the one that advertised this debate. "You have done the church good service in many ways, but my judgement is this is the most valuable book thus far. All Bible students should have a copy", and so on. This is the most valuable book you have published, endorsing it, and many other endorsers. These things are showing the consistency! He claims to be so consistent, and we'll probably have more to say about that. Brother John T. Lewis has written a review of it and exposed it, *but when he did it boomeranged on him and knocked his Sunday School out.*

We do not have time to examine that further now. The Lord being our helper we're going into these things and expose his inconsistencies, the man that claims to be so consistent! Yes, we have many other things that we wish to produce in this discussion. We hope to take up concerning the cup and such as that in just a few monents. Thank you very much.

Porter's First Speech
Second Night — Dec. 5, 1951

Brother Abercrombie, Ladies and Gentlemen:

It gives me pleasure to appear before you again tonight and make a further denial of the affirmation to which you have listened for the past two nights, or the past session last night and for this session thus far this night.

Cecil is still trying to prove that when people come together to be taught by the church they must remain in one group, and be taught by men only, one speaking after another, or one speaking at a time. Now, as I'm engaged in this work tonight, it will be the same manner of work that I was engaged in last night. I'm in the negative of this proposition; therefore, my work is the work of destruction. I'm not trying to prove anything during last night or tonight. I'm merely disproving. Now, for that reason, I'm just taking up the Scriptures he gives and the arguments which he makes. Other scriptures that may be used during the discussion, of course, will come when I get in the affirmative tomorrow night and the following night. But as far as last night is concerned, and as far as tonight is concerned, I'm simply dealing with the arguments which he makes and showing his utter misapplication of those scriptures that he introduces to prove the hobby for which he's been contending all of these years — that the church, the assembly, must remain in one group.

Now, from the statements that have been made by Cecil during this discussion so far, if you were not acquainted with the situation, you would think that we never do any teaching except class teaching, that all the teaching that we do, that my brethren and I do, is simply confined and limited to class teaching, and we never do any other kind. But I want to tell you tonight, respected friends, and most of you know it already, that we do a great deal of teaching with the whole assembly in one group, just as he contends that it all must be done. We do teaching that way every Lord's Day, both morning and night, and upon many other occasions we teach after that method. And yet you would think, from the things that he has been saying, that the only teaching we do is class teaching and that we're using class teaching to try to carry out some of the assemblies that he calls your attention to.

Now, not one passage has he introduced in any of these

assemblies, that confirms the things stated in the proposition tonight. I Believe that the whole group can be taught in one assembly, and we teach that way many times over and over and over from week to week and month to month and year to year. I'm not objecting to teaching being done with an entire congregation in one assembly, but when a man comes along and makes a law that God has not made and says that *you must do it that way,* that *it cannot be done any other way,* as Cecil contends, then I object to *that human law that God hasn't made,* that he has not found in one single passage on the chart that he has had before you those two nights.

I called upon him last night to come tonight and underscore the passage on this chart that, in any form of words, say that *the congregation must remain in one assembly, that they must remain in one group.* Has he done it? Not one single, solitary word did he say about it. What's the matter, Cecil? If all these passages prove that the church must remain in one assembly, and you said "must" meant "must", under the penalty of hell fire, in other words; now if all these passages teach that you must remain in one assembly, then surely, Cecil, you can underscore one of them that says that. Won't you do it for me in your next speech, Cecil? I just wish you would. I'd like to read it to this congregation. Just *one passage,* just *one verse,* you have on your chart that says *one single thing* about the idea that *the congregation must remain* in one assembly. Paul made no such law. God made no such laws contained in any passage on the board or on the chart. That law has been made entirely by brethren who stand with Cecil and for this hobby for which they have been contending all of these years. That is their law; it's a human law that's not found in God's Book. So I'm not objecting to teaching in one group. I'm not objecting to the whole assembly being present, for we often times teach that way from week to week; but I'm objecting to that *human law that he has made* when he says that *it all must be done that way,* for which he has not given one iota of scripture. It just isn't there, and nobody knows it better than Cecil. If it were there, he would have found it a long time before now, but he hasn't; and let me tell you, though I'm not a prophet or the son of a prophet, that when this debate shall have come to a close, he will not have underlined the verse on this chart that say that. Now, you watch and see if my prophecy doesn't come true.

He came back and repeated those in the first part of his speech, 1 Cor. 14:33, "in all assemblies" verse 37, "A commandment"; and then he read down these passages on the chart — 1 Cor. 14:40; Heb. 10:25, Matt. 18:20; Jas. 2:2; Acts 2:6; Acts 20:7-8; Acts 14: 27-28; Acts 15:25-33; Acts 2:1-4; Acts 3:12. And he simply referred to all of them and just asserted that here is no segregation — here is no division; therefore, *all teaching must be done that way*. Well, let's see if you can find that we do teaching that way. Why don't you just conclude that we do it all that way? You find some examples that prove that it's that way.

Incidentally, Cecil, I reminded you last night that the "one leteral cup" brethren will come back to you and say, "Now, in none of these assemblies can you find a plurality of cups", and therefore, they'll say that you *must use one cup*. The passage says "the cup," "a cup," "this cup," and "That cup," and therefore, if you have a plurality of cups, you are a digressive and going to hell. That's what they think about you. The same thing you think about us. And upon the very same ground. They have the very same argument for their "one cup" idea that you have for you "one method of teaching" idea. They stand upon the same basis. They fall together.

Then he came to answering my questions. He said, "Now, I'm going to answer these question. He gave me 15 last night." Yes, but I didn't give them to you all at once. I gave you eight of them in my first speech and insisted that you answer them in your first speech, but you put them off until "tomorrow night". When you did that then I gave you the other seven to go with them, since you were going to answer them tomorrow night anyway. So you had 24 hours to think about these fifteen questions. So he said, "I'm going to answer them, but, of course, he may insist that they are not answered". I have an idea that Cecil felt a guilty conscience along the line about some of them, too, but we're going to look at them anyway and see what we find.

"First: What characteristic must an assembly possess in order to constitute a church assembly?" He says, "I'll accept your definition in the Quincy, Ill., debate." That was a debate I had with Ervin Waters, the "one cup" brother, who will not be fellowshiped by Brother Cecil, and he says that Cecils going to hell upon the same basis upon which Cecil says I'm going to hell, because he says Cecil has no more authority for his plurality of cups than I have for my classes. And he hasn't. They stand or they fall together. They come within the generic term, the generic command. He gets his cups one way, but he won't let me get the classes upon the same basis. They stand or they fall together, but he said, "I'll accept your definition, now, that you gave in the Quincy debate — Matt. 18:20." Did I give that or is that what Waters gave? Did I give that as a definition or was that what Waters gave as a definition, Cecil? Maybe you'd better check into this. I asked Waters that very same question. He's the man that gave the answer. Then after he gave the answer I said, "Well, I'll accept what you said about it." I'm willing to do that , but Waters was the one that gave the definition, not Porter. I merely accepted the definition which he gave, and you knew that, didn't you, Cecil? You knew that, but you didn't say it that way, did you? So, sir. Cecil knew that, but he didn't say it that way. He wanted to make you think that I took the initiative in it, you see, and so he's fighting above board about everything, don't you see? Yes, sir. Now, then, Cecil, since you say you'll accept that, Matt. 18:20 reads, "Where two or three are gathered together in my name", Jesus says, "I'll be with you". And now he says, "I'll accept that as a definition of a church assembly." All right, suppose those two or three are women, Cecil. Would it still be a church assembly? *Come on now!* And if so, could they do any teaching? They couldn't ever worship, according to Cecil. We have a church that couldn't worship, a church that couldn't teach, or just what about it, anyway? You accepted an all-woman church as sure as you're born. You know, he talked about one a while ago. Now, Cecil has already accepted an all-woman church, for he says "where two or three are gathered together", that's a church assembly. A church assembly, if you please, and those two or three could very easily be women, couldn't they, Cecil? If they were, would you have an all-woman church assembly? Huh? What about it, Cecil? Didn't you see what you were getting into? No, he didn't see that. He sees it now, though. So Cecil has gone for an all-woman church assembly. Don't you see? Thank you, Cecil. You're very generous.

All right, the second: "Is a Bible class, or a Sunday School class, a church assembly?" He said, "Since you say that 1 Cor. 14 applied to them all, then it would be." Well, *do you accept it?* I take it that you mean that you'll accept that as a definition of it, — that a Bible class, or a Sunday School class, is a church assembly. He didn't say in so many words that he would, but he said, "Since you say so and so." Do you mean that you'll accept me on that, too? That's what you said about the other one. Now, come back and tell me in your next speech if you mean that you'll accept that; that you'll accept the idea that a Sunday School class, as you call it, or a Bible class, is a church assembly. Tell me in your next speech, Cecil, you didn't tell me. You just said, "Since you say so and so, it must be, according to you". Well, how about it, *according to Cecil?* That's what I want to know. I know what it is, according to me. I'm asking what it is, according to Cecil. What does Cecil say about it? And Cecil didn't tell us. Why didn't you answer it, Cecil? You knew you didn't answer that. Yes, Cecil knew he didn't answer that.

"Number Three: Is it a sin to divide the church assembly?" He said, "It's sinful if you divide it into classes for teaching", but it's not sinful to divide for something else, then, is it? Therefore, the whole argument he made that it is a sin to divide the assembly is not true. Why did Cecil evade that question? Why did you say that it's sinful to divide for class teaching but it's not sinful to divide for something else? Because he does the something else — that's why. I'll tell you what. We're going to say that Cecil's preaching sometime at the morning hour. The whole assembly is present. Back of the pulpit is a baptistry filled with water, with dressing rooms on each side. You don't object to a baptistry, do you, Cecil? Here's one in the back filled full of water. Now, you don't object to a baptistry. I didn't think he does. I never heard him make any objection to baptistries. I know his brethren in general don't. And he probably has dressing room. I don't suppose he would object to dressing rooms in conncection with the baptistry. If he does, why, let him say so.

I return to Cecil and his preaching. He gives an invitation for people to obey the gospel, and four people respond. They come down to the front and want to be baptized, and Cecil takes their confession, has them to confess that they believe that Jesus Christ is the Son of God. Not only the two men, but the two women. They actually make *those two women speak in an assembly of the church.* Yes, he does. He has those two women to speak in the assembly of the saints and confess their faith in Jesus as the Son of God; and then when that's done, some sister comes and takes those two women into this dressing room to prepare for their baptism and divides the assembly. And then Cecil takes the men into this room to make preparation for their baptizing, and divides the assembly again. And then he gets ready for the baptizing. He leads one man down into the baptistry and divides the assembly again. So Cecil divides the assembly three times. Therefore, it is not a sin to divide the assembly unless you divide it for the purpose of teaching. You can divide for any other purpose beneath the stars just so you don't divide it for teaching. That's consistency gone to seed, isn't it? No, it's inconsistency gone to seed. All right.

"Number four, how far must some be removed from the others before an assembly becomes divided?" He said, "Some are divided in the same room, others in other rooms, and so on." Well, if it works in your case, doesn't it in mine?

By the way, Cecil, I asked you last night if the teaching program of your proposition covers this assembly that we are engaged in teaching tonight and last night. What did you say about that? This audience has a right to know if your proposition covers this assembly gathered in this building. Your proposition says that "when people come together to be taught by the church they must remain in one group and be taught by men only." But Cecil last night stood here and taught an assembly divided into a number of groups, and has done the same thing tonight. Some were in this room, some were in that room, some were in that one, and some were in the basement, and they were not in one place. They were divided into groups, and Cecil taught them. Yet his proposition says *they must remain in one group.* And as I said last night, I repeat tonight, Cecil has gone to hell on his own proposition. Come back and fix it, Cecil. I pressed that on you last night. Why didn't you say something about it? *Did you forget it?* Well, write it down now and *please don't forget it,* because if you do forget it, I'll have to put it in writing. So if you don't want me to put it in writing, you answer that question for me.

"Number five, are two things ever parallel in one point but not parallel in other points?" He said, "The Sunday School is paralled with the Missionary Society in that they use Matt. 28:19 as their authority for existence," but he said, "They are not parallel in the fact that the Sunday School doesn't send missionaries to a foreign country." Well, that was a long way to go about it to say "yes", wasn't it? It would have been much easier for him just to have said "yes", because that's what he said. That's what the whole thing amounts to. I said, "Are two things over parallel in one point but not parallel in other points?" He could have said "yes", and that would have covered the whole thing, but he said, "Sunday Schools and Missionary Societies are parallel in that they use Matt. 28:19 for their existence, but they are not parallel in that the Sunday School doesn't sent missionaries to a foreign country." Well, then they are parallel in one point, Cecil says, but not in another; so that say "yes" to the question, doesn't it? Thank you, Cecil. We'll use that again before this debate is over, I'm sure.

"Number Six: Can two men scripturally preach from two radio stations operating on different kilocycles in separate rooms of the same building at the same time?" And he said, "In the debate at Quincy, Porter said women may speak over them provided no men are listening." It happened that I asked that question of Ervin Waters. It was my question and his answer, just as it is my question tonight for Cecil. "Can two men scripturally preach from two radio stations operating on different kilocycles in separate rooms of the same building at the same time?" And what answer did he give? "Porter said at Quincy that the women could speak over them if nobody but women were listening." Does that answer the question? Does that tell me whether they can scripturally do it or not? I'm asking you what do you say about it, Cecil? That's the point. *What do you say about it?* What does your brethren say about that? What position are you going to take? Do you say that two men cannot speak over two radio stations operating on different kilocycles in the same rooms of the same building at the same time? *Say it,* Cecil; in your next speech tell us "yes" or "no" about that. You haven't touched it top, edge, side, nor bottom, and this audience knows you haven't. And you know it, Cecil. Well, *come on.* Come on, *deal with it.* In that connection he said, "Porter said that I misrepresented him last night when I said that he said that women couldn't teach a man". And he said, "Well, I don't know what other conclusion I could reach when he made an answer to a statement like that concerning that question. I don't know what other conclusion I could reach". Why, he said, "I've heard him a lot of times say that women could not teach his men in their Sunday Schools."

Is that saying a woman can't teach a man? Well, that's a long way from what you said, Cecil. You said, "Porter says that a woman cannot teach a man." I never said that a woman cannot teach a man. "Oh, but I've heard you say they can't teach men in your Sunday School classes." Well, suppose I did. That's not saying she can't teach a man, is it? That's not saying they cannot teach a man anywhere, is it, Cecil? You implied that I said a woman cannot teach a man anywhere. That was the implication of your statement, *and you know it.* But come on. *Meet the Issue.*

"Number Seven: Can the church scripturally call together a special group for special training?" He said, "I Cor. 14:31, that governs matters of that kind, one speaking at a time, but if it is a Sunday School, no." "Well, suppose it's a Monday School or a Tuesday School or a Saturday School or something of that kind. *Could she?* Or could the church call together a special group for special training? Now, what's wrong, what's wrong with Cecil? Is he just opposing simultaneous teaching? No. No, that's not it. He's not merely opposing simultaneous teaching. He's opposing any kind of group teaching anywhere at any time unless the whole church is assembled in on place. That's the point. Is that right? If it's not, why, you correct me on it. That's what I'm getting from what you say. If that isn't right, you correct me on it. He more or less repudiated the Gospel Tidings by Brothern Shelburne; however, in that very same paper he made a report a short time ago. He won't fellowship them, but he'll send his report to them. And here we have the Church Messenger. This is one that stands identical with your brethren, isn't it? You accept this one, don't you, Cecil? Here's the Church Messenger. This is published by the Knight brothers over at Booneville, Ark., and on page 7 of this issue, March 15, 1950, they have a display ad in it that says: "Bible Instruction Work — Singing School are to be conducted at the 12th and Blackwelder Church of Christ, Oklahoma City, Okla., June 5 to 28th. Instructors: Leland H. Knight and Ralph D. Gage." They are having special groups for special training. Will you accept that, Cecil, or will you reject it? Do you accept it or repudiate it, either one or the other? We want to know where you stand on that. If you repudiate it, all right. We want to know what you say about it.

"Number Eight: Can two groups from different congregations scripturally meet in separate places for simultaneous teaching or worship?" He said, "If they are starting a new congregation, yes, If a class no." That's consistency, isn't it?

"Number Nine: Can two groups from the same congregation scripturally meet at separate places for simultaneous teaching or worship?" He says, "That's the same question." No, it isn't. He said, "See No. 8." He said, "That's the same question." No it isn't. One question says "Can two groups from *two different congregation.*" The other says, "Can two groups from *the same congregation.*" It's not the same question, Cecil. Now, you come back and answer it.

"Number Ten: Does the command to sing ever include the playing of a mechanical instrument?" He said, "An instrument is found in sing like you find divide in teach." And since Cecil says I cannot find divide in teach, therefore, he says sing does not include the instrument. Thank you, Cecil, For that good confession along that line. Cecil has admitted in his answer that the command to sing never includes a mechanical instrument. For he says the command to teach doesn't include the term divide, and they stand or fall together. They stand on the same basis. So Cecil has admitted in that answer that the command to sing does not include a mechanical instrument. As for the other, we'll deal with it when the proper time comes.

"Number Eleven: What percentage of the membership must assemble before it becomes a church assembly?" He said, "Matt. 18:20". That's two or three, you remember. They may be sisters.

"Number Twelve: When the church comes together for the purpose of teaching can a woman do any type of speaking or teaching in this assembly?" He says, "She may sing." I thought it was a shame for a woman to *speak in any church assembly,* according to your application of that passage — that *it's a shame for a woman to do any kind of speaking.* She must absolutely keep silent, and yet Cecil will allow her to sing when the whole church has gathered together at one place at the eleven o'clock worship on Sunday morning, but Paul says in Col. 3:16 and Eph. 5:19 that when we sing we both speak and teach. Therefore when the woman sings she teaches and she speaks, if she does what Paul says, and Cecil say, "She can sing in that assembly." Therefore, Cecil says *that women can both speak and teach in that assembly on Sunday morning at the eleven o'clock worship.* Then why find fault with Porter if he says she can? You say she can. We both say she can; and, therefore, the statement in 1 Cor. 1 is limited to a particular type of teaching as we shall bring out further along in the discussion.

"Number Thirteen: Can a sister scripturally call a group of sisters to her home and teach them?" He says, "if she meets according to Acts 21:9, Titus 2:3-5, yes, but not in church assemblies." Well, if two or three of them meet in their home, is that a church assembly? You said a while ago it was. He said a while ago it was a church assembly if two or three of them meet. Now, you say that she can't call a group of sisters to her home and teach them if it's a church assembly, but she can according to Acts 21:9 and Titus 2:3-5. That's where the daughters of Phillip prophesied and where Paul told women to teach. He said they can do that. She can actually call a group of sisters to her home according to that, but she can't if it's a church assembly. Now, if she calls a group of sisters, say 15, 20, 30, or 40, whatever it is, to her home and teaches them and that doesn't become a church assembly, then I want to know what characteristic must be added to it to make it a church assembly. That's what I'm getting at. He'll not tell you. You wait and see if he does.

"Number Fifteen: Since a plurality of singers may sing at the same time without causing confusion, why cannot a plurality of speakers speak at the same time without causing such?" He said, "Well, we are commanded to sing as in Col. 3 and Eph. 5, but the speakers were told to speak one by one, and that's the difference." That doesn't say anything about the confusion. I said, "Why can a number of singers sing at the same time and not cause confusion, but if speakers speak at the same time that causes confusion?" "Now, what's the difference between that? The mere fact that it's commanded wouldn't *eliminate the confusion.* The confusion would be there just the same if God commanded one and prohibited the other. *You'd have the confusion just the same.* Well, I want to know what would make confusion on one hand and not confusion on the other. If more than one speaker spoke at once, or more than one singer sang at once, what's the difference? There's a difference, but Cecil's not going to tell you. You wait and see. (I have about three or four minutes?)

That covers nearly everything. We come down now. He goes back to 1 Cor. 14:31, to do away with the classifying, and verses 34-35, "not permitted to speak." But I have already dealt with that just now about the women singing.

"Porter tried to have some sport last night and dealt in things unbecoming." It's unbecoming for me to ask Cecil a question, don't you see? I wonder what he thinks debates are for. It's unbecoming for me to get over here and ask Cecil to tell me "yes" or "no" on the propostion. It's unbecoming Yes, sir, Porter dealt in things unbecoming last night, and that's what he referred to when I pressed him to give us an answer about the charge he had made concerning me. And then I dealt with his charge — his misrepresentation of me — with respect to women teaching men.

In his last debate with Brother Gus Nichols he received fifty-four questions to answer in one speech. I have an idea that you didn't do a very good job of it, considering what you did with these I gave you.

Then, he says, "If when a woman calls a group together, 150 people respond to the call; and if fifteen of them decide to confess Christ, and then all her boys and her husband who were heretofore unbelievers decide to be baptized, they decide to have them baptized. But the preacher is gone. They try to get in contact with the preacher, and find he's gone. So that leaves them in a predicament." Well, I wonder how must better his situation is. Suppose that four of his sisters are down town, and while they're down town they come in contact with some other women who are not members of the church, and they start talking about the matter of salvation, and these women decide they want to be baptized. Two of the sisters immediately get on the telephone and ring for Cecil, but Cecil's out of town. Now, what are *you* going to do? What are you going to do? He's in the very same predicament that he thought he had me in. So there you are, Cecil. We are right there together. You tell me what you'd do and you'll have an answer for what I'd do. *Come on now. What do you say?*

"J. L. Hines in the Gospel Broadcast," "1 Cor. 14." "At Taft, Tenn., Porter said the Missionary Society is an organization. The Sunday School is not an organization." I said that, and I still maintain that that's so. Then he read from a number of these papers here about the organized Sunday School, superintendents, and various other officer. I'll state this, as I have stated before with regard to the superintendent idea: If some man is appointed to look after some details of a particular work, call him a superintendent or whatever you may, after all it's under the supervision of the elders, the overseers. It's nothing more than a foreman on a lot. It's no more than a janitor, a custodian of the building, building committee, or a song director. But if that's an organization set up with a permanent office placed in it, as superintendent, with other officers, Cecil, I'm against that. And all those that you read there tonight about certain officers, superintendent, assistant superintendent, secretary, and on and on — if that indicated they have an organization, I'm against it just as much as you are, Cecil. I repudiate it. Now, what'll you do with these? I said *I don't believe in an organization* called the Sunday School. I believe in the church doing the work, and it's merely a method of teaching, or rather an arrangement for teaching to be done, and it is not a separate organization whatsoever, and I'm not endorsing any organization, or any officers not revealed in the book of God, as officers in an organization of any kind. But a building committee is not an organization, and the song director is not an organization, a custodian of a building is not an organization and matters of that kind that come within it. Thank you, Ladies and Gentlemen.

Abercrombie's Second Speech
Second Night — December 5, 1951

Ladies and Gentlemen, Worthy Opponent:

It is with great pleasure I stand before you once more to continue the affirmation and examination of the things which you have so kindly listened to.

First I will notice just a few things concerning the questions he only briefly noticed, especially number 1. "I accept your definition given in your debate with Brother Waters at Quincy, which was Matt. 18:20. He said, "I will accept that as a church assembly". Of course he endorsed that. Now then, he talked about a church of three women, when there is no such thing in the word of God. It is not authorized. This is modified by the phrase, *"in the name of the Lord"* meaning by the authority of Jesus Christ. The Lord didn't set up *all women churches of Christ,* and he knows that; and so away goes his little fun.

Concerning "unbecoming", it is really unbecoming to get down into a fellow's face and just talk right in his face, blow your breath in his face, and such as that. That's what I was talking about. I don't get over there and get right down and point my finger, and such as that. That's not debating; that is not honorable controversy, and so I don't practice that. That's all I had reference to, getting right over in an opponent's face.

Now on question two, since you said last night that 1 Cor. 14:31 applied to classes in Sunday School, you defined it as a church assembly. He said, "Will you accept that as a church assembly?" Well, Brother Porter, if it is not the church, tell me what it is. If it is not the church what is it? *He is up here opposing a separate organization.* All right then, if it is the church, he has women teaching in church assemblies, so any way he takes it he's caught. He opposes it as being the church to justify women to teach there, and then on the other hand, he will have to take the position that it is the church. If somebody wanted to put musical instruments in it (a church assembly). That's the way they quibble, dodge, or try to.

Then he mentions the baptistry and the dressing rooms, and talking about such as that. Is that the "dividing" of our proposition? Certainly not. Then did you hear Brother Porter say that he believed that you shouldn't divide the assembly such as this? He won't divide his assembly on Lord's Day at eleven, we'll apply it that way. No, he doesn't believe, or most of his brethren wouldn't divide up the assembly at eleven o'clock. When they have the Lord's Supper they wouldn't divide that up into classes. No! But what does he do? If somebody comes down he takes their confession, then he divides his own assembly, he takes them and they go down into the baptistry and he divides that assembly. Where he said, I wouldn't divide that assembly; most of his brethren say not do that. Brother Gus Nichols hung up a great big chart which said, "Cannot divide the Lord's Day assembly for Breaking of Bread", and then the thing backfires right on him. He divides that assembly and says you can't divide it. That's all beside the point. We are not talking about such a thing as that anyway. It's just a trick of sophistry. It's beside the point, it doesn't pertain to this question whatever.

We notice in question five, "Both are the doctrines and commandments of men". That's one thing he left out. Missionary societies and Sunday School are both the doctrines and commandment of men. Yes Sir!

Now, on question number six, about the two radio stations, Brother Porter further said in his Quincy debate, that that would be *"parallel to two men preaching in two congregations."* What did you use it for? You knew it didn't parallel your Sunday School. If it does, why then you have public Sunday School, and he claims it's private. That's the way he tries to justify his women teaching. But that's his parallel! Why, it's not parallel in anything! Why did he present it? He wouldn't know a parallel if he were to see one. Everything he presents just backfires on him.

Then he talked about the "Church Messenger" and something about some teaching being done over at Oklahoma City. I haven't been there! I don't know just exactly how that is going on but I've talked to a few brethren there, and they just come together in congregational capacity and teach the word of God to everybody that comes, as far as I know they are teaching singing there, nothing wrong in that. God hasn't taught us how exactly to do that, but God has certainly taught us how to teach his word in the assembly and that is the subject of this discussion.

Brother Porter said on number twelve: Concerning singing, the women singing in the congregation, "Thank you and so on", well, now let us notice. Brother Porter parrallels singing and teaching in that place. Now let's see how that reacts on him. He tried to parallel, to get an argument, and then he went away from it saying that the teaching there that Paul had in mind was limited. Well, that's what I say! He gets up here and says, "Why he makes it unlimited, absolute silence". Why I've never done such a thing in this assembly, and everybody knows that I've shown that it is restricted to the teaching and addressing of church assembly in speaking and exhortation, and such as that. He is not talking about singing at all, but that reacts unfavorably to him. In the Lord's Day assembly he exhorts all of his sisters to sing, but he wouldn't let one of them teach in the pulpit for anything. There he makes a distinction. He knows what it teaches. All of that, just quibbles.

Now, then, Brother Porter was asking something about this *called group.* He just touched it lightly, it was too hot for him. Yes Sir! "What would you do?" Why didn't he answer? Brother Porter said in his Quincy debate that if she called a group of men she couldn't teach them. What about that? Something wrong somewhere if a woman can't talk to a man about the Bible! Why can't she do it? Well, Acts 18:26 shows that a woman did teach a man. She didn't do it in a church assembly. Women can do personal, individual, private teaching from an individualistic standpoint, and in the sphere of the home as an individual. They cannot do that, and organize assemblies for church teaching, hold evangelistic meetings and such like things. God did not authorize women to do that.

Here is something very interesting, while we are on this point. Here is a little paper published, (if he can read from papers, I've got some papers, too.) This is the "Torch". We'll set the "Torch" to Brother Porter. We'll see him jump with this. "But the order of the day is for educators". Now this is one of his brethren, Brother Wallace. I believe this is Brother Foy. All right. "The order of the day is for educators among us" (not my brethren) here is something his brethren are doing, "among us to send some outside expert, usually a woman teacher, to teach the teachers in various churches how to teach." How about that? "The churches are expected to pay these women experts now, as they would support preachers in meetings, to teach the teachers how to teach. Very soon, if not even now, we shall have travelling women going from church to church teaching the teachers. Already it has been advertised in connection with meetings that Brother and Sister Blank will assist, this or that church, at such and such a place, in a gospel meeting." My brethren are not the only ones who can get up good things! Oh, he's so consistent though! We're the most inconsistent of all, so says Brother Porter. Now did he mention this? Oh, this is a dandy. Why there is not book put out in years, brethren, that has had such a full endorsement amongst the brethren of the Sunday School Church of Christ. Not a one. Why, it was just like a landslide that endorsed it; God's Woman, by C. R. Nichols, just an avalanche of them. Why, gospel Advocate. Firm Foundation, and just a host of them. I've got sixteen of them listed right here. I don't see Brother Porter's name on here, but he's coming, he'll be consistent one of these days! Yes sir, he'll be consistent, I am sure, after a while. Just give him a little time. It's on the way. This Sunday School propositions, it is organizing a female ministry.

All right, let's see. Their own brethren are alarmed about it. D. S. Ligion, Sound Doctrine, published in Montgomery, July 25, 1942, "I heard a young preacher not long ago in the Wednesday night meeting say that the sisters had the same right to teach publicly as the man. I arose and said if that is true, by the same argument women have the same right to get in the *pulpit* and *preach* the same as the *men* and that we should never object to the churches that allow their women to become *preachers, pastors, evangelists.* This young preacher did not appreciate what I said, but brethren this is where the Church of Christ is drifting". Drifting! We want Brother Porter to produce some scriptures on women teachers. All he would do was just get up and say "Women can sing, and that's *some teaching,* and my proposition says that she can do *some teaching,* and there is some teaching in singing, and that's it." I insisted that he produce the scriptures. Come on out! Bring them out! He wouldn't do it. Brother Lewis, he'll let you! But Brother Lewis said in this thing over here ("God's Woman", by C. R. Nichols) concerning the scriptures that Brother C. R. Nichol used to justify women leading prayer and teaching in the Lord's Day assembly, says "if it doesn't teach that why don't the endorsers of God's Woman say what it does teach." It did away with all the restrictions except "No" — don't you get in the pulpit, that's my place! Get the "no" out of it and they will get in the pulpit. That's the authority for teaching in the Sunday School; that's the reason they don't usurp authority over the men in the Sunday School. It is because the elders say, "Go ahead, sister, that's all right."

I'm anxious to know another thing concerning the supervision of this teaching of sister in the Sunday School classes since men are not allowed in a woman's class. I have right here a paper — one Brother, (Gardner S. Hall — "The Way of Life," Oct., 1944) says "that this teaching ought to be properly supervised, and the elders should visit every class," but according to Brother Porter men can't go into women's classes and she is immune from supervision of the superintendent unless it is a woman superintendent! Talk about consistency in the seed! Why, it hasn't got to the see — that's in the root! My friends, that's the thing this brother is contending for, trying to make you believe that is of God.

He talks a lot about hell in this. He ought to be thinking about such, any man that would twist the scriptures as he has been twisting them. This is a serious question. If my opponent had stuck to the issue — had not insisted that we expose him as we are doing, we would have stayed with the precious word of God. I have proved my proposition. He said he wasn't afraid of his practice; that I'm afraid of mine. Let's see his practice. I'm not afraid of anything that I do. If he can prove it sinful I will lay it down.

But here we notice something. I wish to read this from the American Christian Review. It is written by Brother J. C. Roady. He says, "Will We Be Safe or Sorry." "People wanting the innovations did not ask for all of them at the same time". Notice, and he endorses Brother J. C. Roady — one of his brethren. He did that in the Quincy debate. I'm glad that debate is going to be published. We'll use it to expose Brother Porter and the Cuppers, too. "People wanting the innovations did not ask for all of them at the same time." No, they came at it like this. Just a little Sunday School for the children, that is not asking for much. We would like to have just a little organ to entertain these children, and we will keep it in the Sunday School, and not use it in the worship, and if you will let us organize the Sunday School, that will be the only organization we will ask for. Let us have the choir on Sunday night, we don't ask for it for any other meeting. Let us have a public entertainment in the meeting house about one a month. That is not asking much. We will settle just a few things by majority vote. We will let the elders say most of the time what is right and wrong, but just a few is all we ask and there can't be much harm in that. And step by step they went until people who made the plea. "Where the Bible speaks, we speak; where the Bible is silent, we are silent, "had to step aside and innovations came in galore, and we today reap what was sown then. It wasn't a case of being safe, but it was case of being sorry." Those excellent things from their pen.

Now at this time there are many things we would like to notice in his discussion tonight. We shall continue. We want to look at this superintendent consistency! I've shown that Brother Porter, would disavow them and then he would come to their rescue, and he call that consistency. Women teach men in private, Sunday School is private, and have made a law that says a woman can't teach a man in Sunday School. He call that consistency! We are noticing some consistency (?) from those quarters. Sunday School is private — he admits women can teach in private, but at the church women cannot teach men there in the Sunday School, and yet he says it's private where women can teach. Why, he knows that it is an assembly of the church! All right, and the only excuse he has is, "Oh! She might usurp authority over the man in teaching", but the word of God, 1 Tim. 2:11-12 *does not say that a woman can teach just so she doesn't teach a man.* This says, "Let the woman learn in silence with all subjection, but I suffer not a woman to teach, nor" (another thing), "nor to usurp authority over the man", and what's this last phrase down here for? He ignores it entirely — *"but to be in silence."* Now then, look at the consistency!

Now we notice the Cupper consistency. "He took the cup and gave thanks and said, this is my blood of the New Testament which is shed for many for remission of sins." Paul said, "As oft as ye eat this bread and drink this cup". They would have to drink the literal vessel if cup means the container. And he says, "That consistency more than you," Consistency! I believe in the cup, the blood of Christ, the fruit of the vine — that's the one cup. I contend for one cup. I believe in one cup, but it's the fruit of the vine. Why was that injected into this? Just to take up his time! *Gus Nichols even affirmed that cup referred to a vessel. He actually did, and Porter was on the fringe of that false doctrine last night.* I won't charge him with doing it, but he was on the fringe of it. He was desperate for some thing to talk about; (The Cuppers), and Brother Porter preach false doctrine, both are in error. Both have divided the church. *There is no unity with the Cuppers on drinking out of one vessel.* What do they teach? *"You must take a firm stand and preach their false doctrine on the cup",* that's all. It makes no difference whether you drink out of one vessel or not. They won't unite with you on that. You have got to take a *a firm stand* and preach that. It has been demonstrated at Napoleon, Ala. They just had one vessel over there. No! You had to take a *firm stand.*

Porter says there is a conflict between 1 Cor. 14:31 and Acts 15, concerning four teachers — there is just three in 1 Cor. and there is four over in Acts. Just a quibble. Verse 29, "Let the prophets speak two or three and let the others judge." 30th verse, "If anything be revealed to another that sitteth by, let the first hold his peace. For you may *all* prophesy one by one". Three and one equals four, and then he said, *"You may all prophesy",* speaking to the prophets, "one by one that all may learn and all may be comforted." A mere quibble. It doesn't alter the situation whatever. I'm just examining the foolishness he put out.

Now he talks about Paul's ways. Paul said, "My ways, which be in Christ as I teach everywhere in every church." All right, we'll take it from the standpoint of Paul's ways of teaching. Do you ever find Paul using the Sunday School way? He said so. Where will you find it? *Where did Paul use the Sunday School way?* I find in Acts 20:7, here's one of Paul's ways. He was one teacher who did all of the teaching at Troas. That was one of his ways. He did all of the teaching at Troas. That was one of his ways. He did all of the teaching on one occasion. In Acts 15, he was one of four teachers! That's some of his ways — and in Acts 20:20 he taught publicly and from house to house. That's the rest of them. The Sunday School doesn't fit any of them. Paul never organized a Sunday School anywhere.

1 Tim. 2:11-12 — "Does usurp authority" — just mean in church? You know he had a little play over that the other night. No, this is taken care of. "Does usurp authority just mean in church?" He tried to make it appear that I apply that just in church. All right, we find that taken care of in Eph. 5:22-25 — women must be in subjection to man in everything,

Paul says. 1 Peter 3, there are other scriptures showing that a woman is not allowed to usurp authority over man anywhere, and she is prohibited from teaching in church assemblies. Porter's position is that 1 Tim. 2:11-12 allows women to teach in Sunday School just so she teaches no men. This is perverting the scriptures, but does Porter restrict usurping authority only to classes? If so, then she could teach in the Lord's Day assembly at eleven a.m. on Lord's Day, per his twist of this scripture. But does he believe it? No. So I won't charge that. Acts 21:9, Philip had four virgin daughters that prophesied. He said they were prophets. Could they have taught in the presence of their father in their home? Could they teach him in the Sunday School assembly? You know they were not teaching in the church assembly, Paul forbids that.

"Cecil is afraid of his practice." No, I am not afraid of anything that I do. Porter hasn't proven a thing I do to be sinful. I have proved my practice by the scriptures.

Now then we wish to notice something, and here is something that is rich! It comes from the pen of Brother Phillips from Chattanooga, Tenn. W. C. Phillips, "Instrumental Music in Worship", one of the best tracts I ever read and he is a powerful debater when he has the truth. He is as good a debater as you brethren have. But now here's what he says. He was debating musical instruments. "Use made of a chart or a blackboard in teaching, a notebook, a tuning fork, and a time stake in singing, a meeting house, pews or carpets on the floors for the convenience and comfort of Christians when assembled to worship are not now on trial." He's debating musical instruments. That is the position this brother takes when he is debating musical instruments and if you don't believe it, I am turning to the Porter-Tingley debate to show you how he kicked and bucked when another man brings in extraneous or irrelevant matter. "Then he came back to his questions about all those who are in hell" (that was Tingley — this is Porter talking now) "and things of that kind as though that had a thing on earth to do with the proposition. I have shown you from time to time that our question says, that our proposition says, the scriptures teach." that's Porter talking, and he has an adversary that threw in a lot of junk, irrelevant to the proposition. Why, he said, "Look! here is our proposition, our proposition says this, "The scriptures teach — why bring all that in, "just trying to prejudice the people".

Why not stick to the issue, examine the scriptures. It does not say the thing is taught by how many are sent to hell or how many are went to hell or how many are going to hell. That has nothing to do with what the scriptures teach. If everyone of us goes to hell that still does not change the scriptures. I am just trying to get before you what the scriptures say and it matters now how many go to hell as a result of it. Let that be as it may. "The scriptures teach", "That's what I tried to do and he has been trying to hinder me from the beginning of this debate and started off talking about extraneous matter, things that weren't in the proposition.

Let's continue with Brother Phillips. He says, "They are not on trial now. Though it might be proven wrong to use any one or all of these things that does not prove it either right or wrong to use instrumental music in divine worship when Christians are assembled in a church capacity." Sauce for the goose is sauce for the gander! "Reference to any of these things by those who use the instrument in divine praise when trying to defend their practice is simply begging the question and seeking comfort as it is said, "Misery loves company". Any time that I am charged with sinning in anything that I use or anything that I do that is connected with or is pertaining to religious service or Bible teaching, I stand ready to defend the use I make of it and I will not try to prove my right to do it by charging my opponent of doing something for which there is a little or less authority." In other words, I am justified in doing what I am doing because my opponent is inconsistent on a thing or two! "Sauce for the goose is sauce for the gander", Brother Porter says.

Now, many other things we would like to present there, but I turn to 1 John 4:3 (How much time)? Here we have the apostle saying, "Whosoever committeth sin transgesses also the law." I want to mention one other thing lest I forget. Brother Porter said, "Walk up here and find a passage of scripture that says thou must not divide into classes. Find it", he says. Find the scripture that says, "Thou must not divide into classes." All right, let's see how that works out. Porter, put a must in 1 Cor. 14:31. He said those men *must* speak as Paul said there. *And when they speak as Paul said they won't have any classes.* They'll speak one by one unto all. All right, let's trace it just a little further. Can you find a passage that says, *You must not use instruments of music in divine praise?''* Not to save your soul, you couldn't put your finger on one, that said that word for word. That's what he is demanding of me. You know what he is demanding of me. You know what he is working on now? *Whatever is not expressly condemned is allowed. A digressive argument in logic if I ever heard it in my life.* That's what he's working on. That opens the flood gate for every digression. *Whatever is not expressly condemned in so many words, it is allowed!* I have proven by the word of God my proposition. It is sustained. But I continue.

We now turn to Romans 10:17, "Faith comes by hearing and hearing by the word of God.'' Friends, I have presented our practice from the word of God. He can't take the word of God and show his grouping, grading, and segregating of the church, with a plurality of teachers all teaching at once. He will not find one New Testament church of Christ practicing that and this thing right here (Certificate from a Church of Christ in Nashville, Tenn.) shows when it was started by Robert Raikes in 1780, and there's his Sunday School and here's the name of the superintendent of the Sunday School, and there's the name, the Twelfth Ave. Church of Christ in Nashville. They know that's so.

We turn to 2 Cor. 5:7. There the apostle says, "We walk by faith and not by sight.'' I am walking by faith when I do these things. When we practice these things because we have the word of God for our practice. Oh, he says, "We do this a good bit but we don't say that that's the only way it can be done. We do other ways. We do, we endorse this. Friends, there is unity on a "thus saith the Lord,'' there is unity on what the Bible says. "Faith comes by hearing, hearing by the word of God.'' But you *will* never find him producing a New Testament Church of Christ that has anything remotely resembling his practice. I defy him to do it. It cannot be done. He wants me to show word for word. I have shown enough right here — a commandment against it. It forbids classes. (Points to 1 Cor. 14:31 on chart.) And it forbids the women teaching in verses 34 and 35. Now, then we turn and read from another scripture here, 2 Tim. 3:16-17, "All scriptures given by inspiration of God is profitable for doctrine, for reproof, for correction, for instruction in righteousness, that the man of God may be perfect, thoroughly furnished unto every good word.'' The word of God thoroughly furnished us unto every good work, but it left the Sunday School out. He says, reasoning the same way about musical instruments that God gave us complete plans how to work for God, but left the musical instrument out. It left the Sunday School out.

We turn and notice another scripture, 2 Peter 1:3, there the apostle Peter says, "According to his divine power He has given unto us all things that pertain to life and godliness", but he left the Sunday School out. He gave us a divine plan of edifying the church and doing away with confusion. And he has a human plan that he substitutes for God's divine plan, an arrangement added by him to show that he has a better one. I thank you.

Porter's Second Speech
Second Night — December 5, 1951

Brethren, Moderators, Brother Abercrombie, Ladies and Gentlemen:

I am before you now for the closing speech of this session, and of course, the closing speech of this proposition. However, it will not be the closing speech of this subject, because we continue the same subject throughout the debate, except we reverse in the matter of affirmative and negative. The same teaching question goes on tomorrow night and the next night, although during those two session I shall be in the affirmative and Cecil in the negative.

Some two or three things mentioned in his preceding speech that I have in my notes, that I did not quite get to in my other speech, I want to note briefly and go on into the speech to which you have just listened. He said, "During the debate at Taft, Tenn., Brother Porter said that there is not any Singing School in the Bible. Now, find the Singing School in the Bible and I'll find the Sunday School." And he said, "I gave 1 Chron.25:6-7 where they were instructed in song." And then I came along and said that I knew that was there all the time. And he went ahead to show in that connection that they had instruments there; therefore, the instruments and the Sunday School went together. It happen to be that I know something else about that that he didn't tell. In fact, I know it didn't occur as he told it. The matter that was being discussed was as to whether or not the Sunday School *is named in the Bible*, whether you could find the Sunday School named in the Bible. He was arguing that since you could not find "Sunday School" in the Bible, it was unscriptural and anti-scriptural. I said from the same standpoint he could not find "Singing School" in the Bible, and I still say it. The name "Singing School" is not in the Bible, if he will find it I'll find the name "Sunday School" in the very same verse. You find the name "Singing School". That's the point. And I pressed him to give me an example in the Bible that justified *his* Singing School; and he came up with 1 Chron. 25:7-8. That's what he gave. 1 Chron. 25:7-8 justified his Singing School — that was the example that he gave. 1 Chron. 25:7-8. And I turned to the verse before that — not Cecil — but Porter did the turning. I turned to the verse before that and showed that in that school

—82—

of instruction, where they were instructing in singing, they had cymbals, psalteries and harps; and if that justified his Singing School, then it had cymbals, psalteries and harps in it. Cecil came back and said, "I didn't introduce that passage to prove anything." That's what happened, and Cecil knows that it did.

He came to the Gospel Advocate about the rewards and badges and endeavored to prove by that the Sunday School is an organization. Well, does rewards and badges prove it is an organization? Just where does he get that idea anyway?

Then he referred to the paper published by George Henry Peter Showalter and that he had superintendents. "Porter announced his debate in that paper, and that made Porter endorse the whole thing." That seemed to be the gist of his argument, He announced the debate in Gospel Tidings, the paper I read from last night. Those brethren have a nine months' Bible school out there in Kerrville, Texas, and according to him that means he endorsed the nine months' Bible school. Thank you, Cecil.

The Gospel Advocate catalog and some things along that line — the Gospel Advocate literature and the catalogs in which they advertise four minute talks for superintendents, and Sunday School supplies, and so on. And it so happens that the Gospel Advocate also has Baptist manuals for sale. That doesn't mean that I endorse Baptist manuals.

And I spoke about the superintendent a while ago and told you what I believed about that, and if any church has an organization with an officer set up as superintendent and assistant superintendent and secretary and treasurer and things of that kind, I'm just as strong against it as Cecil Abercrombie is. I repudiate those things. Why don't you either endorse or repudiate the things I gave? I'll either endorse or repudiate, but Cecil won't do either.

He came to "God's Woman". He had a great deal to say about that, Brother Nichol's book, and a long list of endorsements. And he said, "Porter's name is not in the endorsement yet, but it will be." Well, wait and see. When it is, well, of course you can bring it up, and let that be as it may. Many men make statements that I do not endorse. I do not know just what is in God's Woman, written by Brother C. R. Nichol. I know that Brother C. R. Nichol is a great preacher of the gospel, but Brother C. R. Nichol *could make a mistake,* the same as I could make a mistake, or the same as Cecil could make a mistake. And if any man makes a mistake, and I know it to be a mistake, I wouldn't endorse it, whether made by Brother C. R. Nichol, or any other man, so far as that goes. I feel sure Brother Nichol would agree with me on this.

And so I justly contend that we are scriptural in arranging into classes or groups for teaching, whether somebody makes some erroneous statement or not.

In the church at Corinth, there were men that taught certain things — that the ressurrection was past already. But that didn't mean that it was so, that Paul endorsed it, and so in regard to many other things along that line.

Now, then, to the speech to which you have just listened. On the questions — number one — Matt. 18:20. That question said, "What characteristics must an assembly possess in order to constitute a church assembly?" The only characteristic he gave was Matt. 18:20. He said, "I accept that definition." I came back and said, "All right, three women assemble. Three women some together or assemble. Is that a church assembly?" He came back and repudiated that and said, "No, that's not a church assembly because Matt. 18:20 is modified by the expression 'in the name of the Lord'. 'In the name of the Lord' modifies that — in the name of the Lord means by the authority of the Lord." I thought you claimed that the Bible authorized the woman to teach women. I thought that's the very thing you claimed. And those women come together. *Can two or three women come together* and do *according to the authority of the Lord? Now, come on.* Can two or three women meet *by the authority* of the Lord in order to teach? Can they teach one another? Can one woman teach two other women by the authority of the Lord? Can they, Cecil? *Come on and tell me.* Wait and see if he does.

"Oh," he said, "all the talk about being unbecoming. It's unbecoming to get over and blow your breath in a fellow's face and point your finger at him." But that's not what was hurting Cecil. The audience that was here last night knows that that hasn't been Cecil's trouble. It wasn't the fact that I was close to him with my breath or my finger or something of that kind. The fact was his seat was getting too warm on that question. That's where his trouble was. It wasn't that. Then, "number two, is a Bible class, or a Sunday School class, a church assembly?" He said, "Now, if it's not a church assembly, then

—84—

what is it?" Well, I'm asking you. What do you say about it Cecil? That's what I've been trying to find out. I know what I thing about it. I'm asking you what you think about it. Is a Bible class, or a Sunday School class, as they are called a church assembly? I want to know. You haven't told us. I want to know. Is it a church assembly?

Then we come to the baptistry and dressing rooms. He said, "I heard Porter say that you shouldn't divide the assembly for the Lord's Supper. And therefore, you have confessions on that occasion, and you divide the church, just as I would if I had someone to respond to the invitation." Yes, but Porter has never arqued that it is a sin to divide the assembly, yet that's been the basic principle upon which you fellows have operated; and that's been your major argument all through the years — that it is a sin to divide the assembly. Now, Cecil backs up on that major thing for which they have been contending throughout the years and says, "No, it's just a sin to divide the assembly under certain circumstances." Well, he's just giving up his major plea all these years. That's the thing I'm talking about.

"Number Five." The parallel between the Sunday School and the Missionary Society. He said they both were doctrines of men.

Then he came on down to the next one. "Can two men scripturally preach from two radio stations operating on different kilocycles in separate rooms of the same building at the same time?" Do you know what Cecil believes about it? Is there a person in this audience who can tell what Cecil believes about that one from what he says? "Can two men scripturally preach from two radio stations operating on different kilocycles in separate rooms of the same building at the same time?" What did Cecil say he believes about that? I wish somebody would tell me. I don't know what he meant. I don't know what he teaches. I don't know what he believes about it. He's never said. I want to know, Cecil, do you believe that two men can do it? Tell us, "yes" or "no". Can two men scripturally preach from two radio stations operating on different kilocycles in separate rooms of the same building at the same time? Tell us about it, Cecil. You haven't told us yet; you haven't told us yet; you haven't answered that question; and you know that you haven't answered it; and this audience knows that you haven't answered it. It's unbecoming though, but he's going to have to suffer a little. Just let it go. We are going to see that that comes before him from time to time.

But he said concerning the Quincy affair "that women couldn't speak over it because there would be men listening. You'd parallel that with preaching. And therefore you parallel it with the Sunday School. Women cannot teach in your Sunday School classes." Well, women couldn't *teach over men* in the Sunday School class any more than they would in the other assemblies of the church. That's the thing I have contended for all the time. When she teaches over the radio to a mixed multitude of people, when she teaches before an audience gathered like this tonight, *she is certainly teaching over men.* And that's the thing the Bible doesn't permit her to do. But when she teaches her own sex in a Sunday School class, or Bible Class, *she is not teaching over a man.* We'll have more about that directly in the regular order because it came up again in Cecil's speech.

Regarding the statement from the Church Messenger which I read, he says, "I haven't been there, and I don't know, but I am supposing that everybody comes — as far as I know everybody comes — to those groups." Well, it so happens that he supposes wrong. They invite the young men to come to those groups. They have a special course for young men, and the young men are the one who are urged to come to those groups. They come from various states over the country. Not only around Oklahoma City, but they come from various other states. The young men come to those training schools. That's from the Church Messenger. Now, Cecil, either endorse or repudiate it, one or the other. But since he admitted a while ago that things can be parallel in one point and not parallel in others — then when I say that radio preaching is parallel with Sunday Schools I simply meant it was parallel in one point, in the point of simultaneous teaching. That's the point. In radio preaching — two men from separate radio stations in the same building on different kilocycles — you have two men speaking simultaneously to different audiences. That's the thing you have in Bible classes. You have two teachers or a dozen teachers to different audiences, not two teachers in one group; not two teachers to one audience, but to different audiences. *In that way they are parallel.* He's objecting to *simultaneous teaching,* teaching at the same time in different rooms of the same building. He's not objecting any longer to the dividing of the assembly. It's whether or not you teach after you divide the assembly. That's the point. It's not the dividing of the assembly that he objects to any more; it's whether you have teaching after you divide the assembly. And if you have simultaneous teaching; that is, teaching going on at the same time in two different places, then it's wrong. That's what you have on the radio stations if you have two men speaking on two radio stations operating on different kilocycles in separate rooms of the same building at the same time. Now, you tell us whether or not you could do that.

On "number twelve", he said, "Porter paralleled sing and teach", and that he admits that teaching and speaking are limited there, and she is not permitted to speak about the things that you — men-are talking about, but she can sing. I said *singing is not prohibited.*" All right then, *all speaking in assemblies on the part of women is not prohibited,* is it, Cecil? I'll try not to blow my breath in your face, but I'll somewhat turn this way. Cecil, then you admit, in that acknowledgment, that *all teaching and all speaking in the assembly on the part of women are not prohibited, won't you?* That's what you mean, isn't it? That's it, isn't it? Come on, let's shake hands on that. That's what you said, isn't it? *Didn't you say that?* Won't you stand by it? That's what he said, that it does not prohibit all speaking and all teaching. Well, it is not a sin for women to speak in song, is it? A woman, therefore, can speak without it's being a shame — a woman can teach without it's being a shame, because he says she can both speak and teach in the regular worship assembly on Sunday meeting. *Women can do that.* Yes, sir, he said so. Well, he said, "Porter believes that". Why, certainly I do. Certainly I believe it. Cecil does too. That's what I'm getting at. We're agreed on that, aren't we, Cecil? Therefore, he doen't believe that I Cor. 14 prohibits all types of teaching. And we know the type that it does prohibit is the type that is discussed in the context. That's what he said. And the context makes no prohibition about a woman teaching her own sex. Therefore, if a woman teaches her own sex, it does not violate the teaching prohibited in I Cor. 14. There you are. She's not violating I Cor. 14 if she is teaching her own sex. The teaching that there is considered is according to verse 23, when the whole church comes together and that she must be in subjection to man in her teaching. If she is not in subjection to men, it is prohibited in I Cor. 14. If she got up and preached to an audience, as a public preacher, she would not be in subjection to men; therefore she is violating I Tim. 2:12, that says she is "not to teach nor usurp authority over the man". So I Cor. 14 prohibits her from teaching in certain capacities. It does not prohibit her from speaking in songs, or teaching in songs, nor does it prohibit her from teaching her own sex. It just isn't there. He limits it, but he doesn't want me to limit it. He won't take it in an unlimited way, but he wants me to.

He said, regarding the Quincy affair, the called group in the Quincy debate — if they called a group of men, could she teach them? Porter said, "No." Well, for the very same reason she couldn't speak to a congregation of men here or anywhere else. She would be teaching "over the man". That's why I said it. But he said in Acts 18:26 she did teach a man. Yes, I believe she can teach a man. Why, certainly so; I never said she couldn't do that. Well, more of that in a little later time, I think, in the notes.

Then he came to the Torch by Brother Wallace regarding the order of the day to send out women teachers to teach teachers how to teach, and if this thing goes on, they will be traveling evangelists, and they will be being called for gospel meetings, and things of that kind. And Cecil, I take the very same stand upon that that Foy E. Wallace took. I stand with Foy E. Wallace upon that. I'm against women preachers, women evangelists, and against the idea of sending out women teachers to teach teachers how to teach. And, of course, he implied in that the teaching of men teachers how to teach, and then sending them out as evangelists in the field to preach the gospel just as men preach it now. I'm certainly against that, and if any of my brethren are doing it, I'm just as much against them as I am against this silly thing for which Cecil is contending. Just as much.

"Brother D. S. Ligon in the paper, Sound Doctrine, said he heard a young preacher say the women had the same right as men did to do teaching. And we're drifting." Well, when a man does that he's drifting. I certainly admit that. But I'm not contending for that; so I'm not drifting yet. You're meeting Porter this time, Cecil. All right.

Regarding the debate in — oh, yes, he said in the debate on women in Taft, Porter didn't make any effort to prove anything about women teachers. He said the only thing that he would do would be to just bring the matter of singing, and said that they can sing, they can sing, they can sing. That singing is teaching, and singing is speaking; that was all that Porter introduced. And yet before he sat down he brought up I Tim. 2:12 and gave Porter's application of that. What's the matter, Cecil? One time he said the only thing on earth Porter introduced was just that women could sing, and then turned right around and gave Porter's application of I Tim. 2:10-12. Something's wrong. Something's wrong. Well, we'll see, before this debate is over, something that he had at Taft, Tenn. Something that he didn't say anything about. But I daresay you'll not make any effort to reply to it this time. You wait, we're not through with this discussion yet.

One brother said that elders ought to supervise women's classes — that would put women teaching in the presence of men. I wonder if the elders couldn't supervise women teachers without sitting in their classes and listening to them teach all the time.

Well, he said one thing about it, "Porter ought to be thinking about hell, because he's twisting the scriptures so." The feeling's mutual, Cecil.

"Brother J. C. Roady in the American Christian Review," note he said, "Will We Be Safe or Sorry?" and that we didn't ask for all the innovations at one time, but just a little here, a little there, an organ here and a Sunday School there, and so on and so on, and finally got them all, including the plurality of cups. We've discussed, however, the superintendent matter, but he's at it again.

Then he makes these efforts to prove Porter's inconsistency; that Porter said his Sunday School is private teaching; he says a woman can teach in private but she cannot teach them in a Sunday School class. Therefore the Sunday School class must be public. I never told Cecil whether I thought the Sunday School class was public or private. I never told him anything about how I thought about that. He's never asked me except in a round-about way. And I have said this, if you'll tell me what you mean by public or private, I'll tell you what your answer is. I think Brother Ervin Waters asked that question. Are classes private or public? Tell me what you mean by "private". Tell me what you mean by "public". If by "public" you mean everybody's invited to that class, then certainly it is not public. Because everybody's not invited to that class. Why, the very term "class" restricts. There would be no such use of the term, there couldn't be any such term, if there wasn't any restrictions. If you mean by "public" that everybody is invited, everybody's not invited to any one particular class. And so from that standpoint, if that's what you mean, it would be private. But when I said that a woman can teach in private I didn't say she could teach in private *under all circumstances*. There are some circumstances involved under which a woman could teach — that doesn't mean that she can teach just so a thing is private, that she can always teach because it's private. There are other things governing the matter besides the idea of it's being private. I Tim. 2:12 for an example. I Tim 2:11-12 doesn't say she cannot teach a man. No, and you never heard Porter use that to prove she cannot teach a man.

Then again the "Cuppers". Now, regarding this cup, Jesus said, "This is my blood. Now eat of this and drink of this." He doesn't mean the literal vessel. I know, Cecil; I know all those arguments. You're not telling me anything about that, but I'm still insisting that we have the very same principle upon which you're operating — that the Bible says "the cup," and "a cup", and "this cup", and "that cup". And you can't have a liquid without having a container, can you, Cecil? You've heard the argument. You can't have a liquid without having a container. If you have "the cup", and that means the contents, you must have the contents in a cup, don't you see? And therefore it is said that there must be just one literal container, and there was no division on that until the plurality came along. You know a while ago he said there was no division on this matter until you fellows started the classes. Well, there was no division between you and the other fellows until somebody started the plurality of cups, you see. So that puts you right back in the boat with me. We're riding together.

I Cor. 14:31 and Acts 15. He said, "Porter said these were in conflict." No, Porter didn't say that. I said, according to Cecil's application of them, they are in conflict. For he makes I Cor. 14 cover the whole teaching program of the church. And I Cor. 14 mentions only two or three — prophesy two or three. But in Acts 15 we have four teachers teaching instead of two or three. He came back and said three and one makes four. Yes, but you don't get three and one — you added one. It said two or three. Two and three would make five, but it didn't say two *and* three, but two *or* three. I said if your application of it is true, if this covers the whole teaching program of the church, then you have it in conflict. Porter didn't say it was in conflict. I don't believe I Cor. 14 covers the whole teaching program of the church.

Regarding I Cor. 4:17 — Paul's ways. Paul mentioned "my ways, as I teach in every church." I called your attention last night to the fact that he said "my ways", for Cecil said there was just one way. He came back in answer to this and said (Porter looks at notes). Oh, here it is. "Yes, Paul had ways, one time he did all the teaching, another time he was one of four. That's two different ways." Well, in both places they simply spoke to the audience by the lecture method, didn't they? They got up and addressed the audience just like we're doing now, the same method, the same way. In the case of one, there was just one speaker speaking to the assembly; and in the case of the other, there were four speakers all following the same way. It wasn't two different ways. Just four speakers following the same way. That was all. And so he still just has one way that Paul taught. Well, then your passage is wrong. You'll have to hunt something else, so far as your proposition is concerned.

But in I Tim. 2:12, the authority over the man, he claimed Porter said that would have to be just in the assembly. "No," he said, "we can read Eph. 5:22 — she must be subject to man in everything." Well, I believe all of that. I was showing the misapplication he made of the passage. You said when Paul said, "I suffer not a woman to teach" in that passage he referred to teaching in church assemblies. I said if that be true, then the rest of it referred to church assemblies, too. And it said, "nor to have authority over the man." If teach means in church assemblies, having authority over the man means in church assemblies. It's all right there together. And so if that means she can teach anywhere else except in church asemblies, then that means she can exercise authority over the man anywhere else, except in church assemblies. I said, "Cecil's misapplication of the passage." He seemed not to get the point.

Acts 21:9 — the daughters of Phillip that prophesied — Could they have taught in the presence of their father in their home? In the case that they could, could they not have taught in classes? Now, they taught before somebody. There was prophesying done. I'm certain that they didn't prophesy or do the teaching to their own children in their home because they were virgins. I just wonder where the teaching was done.

And then Brother Phillips' tract, W. C. Phillips, on Instrumental Music. The blackboard and things of that kind are not on trial, or any man that is injecting these things is begging the question when he's meeting an instrumental music fellow. So he claims I am begging the question tonight. Well, I am certain that he's begging the question concerning these things that are encountered just here. But let us look at it. If I am meeting an instrumental music fellow, when he tried to make a parallel out of his instruments of music with my song book, do you know what I would do? I would set about immediately to show they are not parrallel. And if he proved, Cecil, that the instrument of music is parallel with the song book, both you and I are sunk. We are, if he proves that; we are both sunk. And so from the same standpoint I am showing that your position on the cup is parrallel with my position on the class, and it's your duty to prove they are not parallel; and if you don't, you're sunk. I give you the privilege to try your hand at that.

I wanted him to find the scripture on the chart of any verse that said we must remain in an undivided assembly. And he said here it is — I Cor. 14:31, "You may all prophesy one by one, that all may learn, and all may be comforted." He said that prohibits classes — that prohibits any other group, for you may all prophesy one by one, all speaking to one assembly. Why, we never violated that. I am still contending that we never have but one teacher to one group — one teach to one assembly. *Let him prove to the contrary.* Has he tried to do it? Not on your life, he hasn't. He'll not try to do it. We have only one teacher to one group, and that concerns only one group, and it doesn't say a word about having other groups or anything of the kind. It just isn't there.

"Oh", but he says, "you can't find 'you must not use an instrument of music'." Well, you've got your "must not" put on a par with "must". You're the man that puts a "must" in there, and you said it was specific and strong. And that the Lord made it "must". You said it's there-that *they must remain in one assembly.* And you said the Lord made that law-that the Lord said it must be done. All right, you're the man that said it must be. Now, give us the "must". I Cor. 14:31

doesn't contain it. No, I'm not arguing that everything is accepted that is not prohibited in so may words. He's confusing "must not" with "must". We're making an argument upon the term "must"; he said it "must" be that way. All right, since he said it *must be that way,* why, then, of course, you must produce that passage that says so, or he's made a law where God hasn't made it. That's exactly what he's done. Do I have about one or two minutes? Moderator: "One Minute'.

That brings us down to these last passages over here, II Cor. 5:7, "walking by faith," and II Tim. 3:16-17, "every good work" is authorized. II Pet. 1:3, where we have everything that "pertains to life and godliness". And since a plurality of cups is not mentioned, according to him, we are not walking by faith if we use them, and it's not a good work, and it doesn't pertain to life and godliness. Thank you Cecil, we're right in the same boat together again, sailing down the same stream. In the same boat together again, Cecil, Yes, if it's sauce for the goose, it's sauce for the gander.

Now, I thank you very kindly for your attention tonight. I trust you will take these things home and read your Bibles and see whether these things are so, and come back tomorrow night and the next night, and we'll take up the other side of the question and have other scripture to investigate before the debate comes to a close. I thank you very kindly.

Porter's First Affirmative Speech
Third Night, December 6, 1951

Brethren Moderators, Brother Abercrombie, Ladies and Gentlemen:

I am grateful again for another privilege of appearing in your presence to go into a further discussion of those things revealed in God's eternal truth. The proposition, which has just been read in your hearing, I believe with all of my heart. I have therefore committed myself to the affirmation of the things involved in that proposition.

The rules of debate require that we define the terms of the proposition that there be no mistake regarding their meaning. However, this proposition is so simply arranged, the words are so easily understood, that it seems that very little difinition would be required, but if there must be some definition I would simply state this. The proposition says that "the practice of arranging into groups the people who come together to be taught by the church". By that statement we simply mean, of course, arranging into what we call classes, or groups, at various places for the teaching that is to be done by the church, the teaching of the truth of Almighty God. And "using both men and women to teach these groups" simply means that the men may teach some of the classes, and the women may teach some of the other classes or groups; and not that the women can teach all of them, but some of them can be taught by the women. And, furthermore, that this "practice" is authorized by the scriptures." Of course, by the "scriptures" we mean the word of God, the Bible. And it is "authorized by the scriptures" in that it is in harmony with scriptural teaching and scriptural principles, as I shall endeavor to show during the progress of the discussion tonight. I deem that that's sufficient so far as the definition of terms is concerned. So I pass on to a consideration of some things in this connection.

It is almost impossible, of course, for a man to take notes after a speaker and then follow those notes so closely that he would not miss a point now and then. So in checking over my notes today I found some two or three points what I looked in my speech last night. Since we are continuing a study of the very same question for these two remaining nights, I want to note briefly some three or four points along that line before proceeding with my affirmative arguments.

One thing in particular that Cecil mentioned last night was that we never tell how many of our preachers leave our position for theirs. I mentioned that many of the preachers were seeing through that school program, that Bible school being conducted at Kerrville, Texas, and were giving up the anti-class position. He said we never tell how many of our preachers are leaving to take their stand with them. Well, I'll leave that for him to tell. And to show you that I was not mistaken about that, I want to read a statement or two from the paper here. This is the "Church Messenger" published at Booneville, Arkansas, by Paul Knight. Regarding those who had left them and taken their stand with us in recent years, he says,

"One by one those lined up with you, working with you, and publicly proclaiming the merits of the Kerrville work, have shown your true colors. Take J. V. Davis, Rex Kimbrough, L. Hayhurst, D. L. Shelton, J. F. Lilly." And then, he says, "Now two more, Dennis Kellog and Norman Gipson."

Now, here in this one paper he has mentioned seven of the preachers who recently left the anti-class group to take their stands with us, and there are others, some of whose names I could call that are not mentioned in this paper.

Another thing he referred last night to the Tingley debate, and argued that Poster is following the same course in this debate that he condemned in Tingley: that I said that it made no difference how many people went to hell as a result of the truthfulness of the propostion, that didn't disprove it. And I still say the same thing; and I am not occupying the position here that Tingley occupied there. I am not trying to prove that his position is wrong because it sends somebody to hell. I was merely trying to find out how strong he made the word "must". That was all. And besides, the things that Tingley brought in concerned other religious bodies all over the country that were not involved in the debate, but the statements I made have involved nobody but the two groups that are engaged in this discussion. So the cases are certainly not parallel.

Another thing, I have asked him time and time again — I was to re-emphasize it tonight — Cecil, can you, in view of your proposition that you have affirmed for the past two nights, scripturally teach the people who have been gathered in these audiences? Your proposition said that when people come together to be taught by the church *they must remain in one group.* I said last night and night before that these audiences have not remained in one group. We have had them in the auditorium. We have had them in the various rooms of the basement round about. They've been in different places. They *have not remained in one group,* and yet Cecil has been teaching both nights under a situation of that kind. He hasn't said a word about it. I'm pleading with him to tell me something about it. The audience has a right to know something about it. And certainly, in justice to truth and in fairness to truth, Cecil ought to come right out and tell us something about it. Cecil, can you scripturally speak to congregations arranged as these have been the past two nights? Now, don't forget to tell us about it. I don't want to have to give it to you in writing. I am sure you can write it down. So please tell us about it. You have been doing it for the past two nights. What are you going to say about it?

And then another thing, regarding the woman's church, the "all women's church" at Montevallo, Ala., Cecil talked about something that he didn't know very much about. The fact of the case is that there is a women's college there, a state school, and a number of members of the church are attend-school there. In order to have worship, their worship is conducted there; but so far as is known there has always been a man there to conduct their worship and to take the lead in that thing.

And then, one more thing. I want to emphasize again, as I've emphasized before, that *much of our teaching is done with the whole congregation in one assembly.* You may get the idea from what Cecil has said from time to time that we never follow any other plan of teaching but class teaching, but I offer the assertion — I'm not in fear of it's being disproved — that *we do 100 times as much teaching to groups that are assembled in one place as Cecil and his group do.* Yes, sir, I believe I could stand upon that — that we do 100 times as much of that kind of teaching as his group does. And so all that he said along that line that indicated that we had only class teaching certainly isn't true.

Now, then, to the affirmative arguments. My first affirmative argument is going to be based upon some matters that pertain to generic terms or generic commandments.

Sometimes the Lord gives commandments in generic terms, and those commandments involve the means that are necessary to do those things in an orderly manner. In other words, the means of doing a thing are involved in the command to do the thing. And so I call your attention to the board.

Chart number one. Over on this side I have No. 1, the word "Go." God demands it. Matt. 28:19. He said to the apostles, "Go ye therefore, and teach all nations." Here is a commandment; here is a generic term that says "go". "Go therefore, and teach all nations." All we have various means by which that commandment might be obeyed that are not specified in the New Testament — things that can be done in the carrying out of that command, but are not specifically mentioned. God said "Go", but God did not put a limit on it as to "how" they go, for there are various methods of travel. There are various means of conveyance. In view of that commandment, men might walk, or they might swim, or they might skate, or they might ride. These are just some of the forms of going. If a man walks, he still would be doing what the Lord said. The Lord said, "Go". If they walked, they're going. That's what the Lord said do, and they are not doing anything the Lord did not say do when the Lord said, "Go". If a man should even swim across a stream somewhere to get to his appointment, he is still doing what the Lord said. The Lord said, "Go", and that is one method of going. That's one means of doing what the Lord commanded. Furthermore, the same could be said about skating or about riding; and, of course, the word "ride" is a broad term. It includes many forms of riding. It might be on horseback, or on the back of a donkey. It might be in a boat. It might be in an automobile. It might be in a buggy. It might be in an airplane. It might be on a bicycle. There are many ways that a man can ride. Why, the Bible no where says anything about an automobile or an airplane or a bicycle, yet we believe that men could go on a bicycle, or on an airplane, or in an automobile, and be doing what the Lord said. The means of doing a thing *is* involved in the command to do it. So when they "go" they're just doing what the Lord said. Whether they walk, swim, skate, ride, or however they go, they're doing what the Lord said do; for the command to "go" includes the means by which the going may be done, and, therefore, the means becomes scriptural, inasmuch as it is involved in the command that said to "go".

Now, some man could jump up and start a hobby on that like these brethren have started on the class situation; and they could say, "I don't read anything in the Bible about an airplane, or a bicycle. Where did you ever read of the apostle Paul riding on a bicycle or the apostle Peter taking a trip in an airplane to fill an appointment? The Bible said nothing about those things; therefore, you can't do them. You are under condemnation. You're anti-scriptural, and you're going to hell if you do it." Well, the fact is that the command to "go" includes the methods and the means by which the going is done.

Then in the second place, we have another word in the same connection, "Baptize". "Go ye therefore and teach all nations, baptizing them." Here is the command to "baptize". It is also a generic term, and that command to "baptize" involves the various means by which the baptizing may be done. It may be done in a river. It may be in a lake. It may be in a pool, or it may be in a baptistry. If men baptize in the river, they're going what the Lord said. If they baptize in a lake or a pool, they're doing what the Lord said. They're just "baptizing". If they baptize in a baptistry, they're doing what the Lord said. The Lord said "baptize". Although the book of God doesn't mention a baptistry, it says nothing about anybody ever having been baptized in one, but it's a means of doing what the Lord said to do, and, therefore, a baptistry is involved, or included, in the command to "baptize". And when men are baptized in a baptistry, they're being baptized scripturally. Such is authorized by the scriptures because the command to baptize, involves the means by which the thing may be done.

And so over here again, in the third place, we have the commandment to "sing". Eph. 5:19 — "Speaking to yourselves in psalms, and spiritual songs, singing and making melody in your heart to the Lord." All right, here in singing. The Lord commands us to "sing", and there are the means by which that singing may be done. You may use song books as a means; you may use voice parts; and you have to use some voice part, of course. But it may be one, or it may be another. It may be soprano, alto, bass, or tenor; and, at the same time, it may be done in singing schools, or you may even sing an invitation song. These are all things involved in the command to "sing". And yet song books, voice parts, singing schools, or invitation songs are not mentioned in all the New Testament. We don't find where they ever did those things, so far as any specific record is concerned. Where can you read in the Bible that they sang an invitation song? Where can you read in the Bible that they used a song book? Where can you read in the Bible, that they sang bass, soprano, alto, or tenor, or things of this kind? It just isn't there. Yet these things are included in the scriptural requirement to "sing", because the command to "sing", being a generic command, involves the means by which the command may be obeyed.

In the fourth place, we have the word, "Teach". Matt. 28:19, the same passage again: "Go ye therefore and teach all nations". We are limited as to what we teach. In Mark 16:15, they were told to preach the gospel; in I Peter 4:11 to speak as the oracles of God speak. So we are limited as to what we teach; and yet "teaching" is a generic term and involves the various means or methods by which the teaching may be done, just as with respect to these other things. So if a man "teaches" from the pulpit, as I am doing tonight, he is doing what the Lord said. He is teaching. If he uses a printing press in order to print literature and send out over the world, he is teaching. That's what the Lord said do. If he preaches over a radio, he is still doing what the Lord said. The Lord said, "Teach." If he preaches from a chart or a blackboard, he's doing what the Lord said. The Lord said, "Teach". And if he teaches in classes, he's still doing what the Lord said. The Lord said, "Teach". And the man who teaches in classes is no more violating what the Lord said than the man who uses the printing press, the radio, or the chart, for you'll find none of them mentioned in the New Testament. The book of God says nothing about "printing presses". It says nothing about "radio", nothing about "charts", nothing about "classes" in so far as the actual word is concerned in that connection. Therefore, we have these as means of doing what the Lord said, and consequently when we follow those means of doing what the Lord said, we are simply obeying the Lord's commandment.

My brethren on the opposing side claim that "classes" is a violation of the teaching and regulations laid down in the book of God. *But it is only a means of doing what the Lord said.* Just as "go" involves the means of riding when men ride they are doing what the Lord said — so "teach" involves the means of teaching. And when it is done in classes, that's only an arrangement by which teaching is done, and nothing is done there that the Lord did not say here to do. "Teach". That's what the Lord said, and it is nothing more than when men preach over the radio. They are still teaching. The Lord said, "Teach". And so all of these as means are included in the commandment to teach. Consequently, we have all these things authorized by the scriptures, though they are not specifically mentioned there in so many words. Yet they come within the scope of the commandment that said to "teach", and, consequently, can be done scripturally. And on that point Cecil admitted last night at least, that he could scripturally preach over a radio.

And then number five, we have the word, "Play". I've used this parallel because it has been contended by my opposing brethren that our class teaching is on parallel with the using of instrumental music in worship. I want to show you tonight that there is no parallel there at all. So far as the "play" and the "classes" are concerned, there is a parallel. Go, baptize, sing, teach, play, are all parallel in that they are *co-ordinate terms*. They are not parallel in the fact that the *first four of them are commanded,* but the *fifth one is not commanded.* And so in that case they are not parallel. But they are parallel in that they are co-ordinate terms; and each of them, if the Lord had commanded (pointing to word "play") this, would stand upon the same ground as all the rest. You would have means by which it could be done: and if the Lord had said, "Play" in praise to God, then that would authorize the organ, or harp, or the banjo, or the violin, or any other instrument, that might be used as a means of doing what the Lord would say, in case the Lord said that. All right, then we have the "organ" bearing the same relationship to "play" that the "classes" bear to "teach", or that the "song books" bear to "sing", or that the "baptistry" does to "baptize", or "riding in an automobile" would to "go". Those things are all parallel in that respect. But classes, teaching in classes, is just a *means* of doing *what the Lord said* — nothing but teaching. But *playing on an organ is not doing what the Lord said* when he said, "Sing", or when he said, "Teach". Those things are not parallel. These are means (pointing to no. 5 on board) of doing this particular thing, "Play". But here we have (pointing to means of "sing") *means* of *singing,* and you cannot put this (pointing to means of "play") up in this place and make them a *means of singing.* In other words, *play* us *not a means* of *singing,* but *song books are a means of singing.* Singing schools and voice parts become *means* of *singings*. Singing schools and voice parts yes, but these others down here (pointing to "play" and to instruments) cannot be any means of singing whatsoever, and, therefore, they are not parallel.

But I pass on. In the second place. I want to call your attention to a statement made in the Old Testament that's a parallel with this system that we have before us tonight. I want to go to Exodus, 18th chapter, and I want to call attention first to the fact that in Deut. 6:7 God commanded Israel to "teach". And sometimes we find, according to Deut. 13:11-15, that they taught in one assembly. yes, once every seven years according to that arrangement they taught in an assembly with everybody in one assembly. But all teaching was not done that way. God commanded to teach, and there were various means and arrangements involved in the teaching; and so I go to Exodus 18 to show you something that existed there. Beginning with verse 13 of this chapter we read: "And it came to pass on the morrow, that Moses sat to judge the people; and the people stood by Moses from morning unto the evening. And when Moses' father-in-law saw all that he did to the people, he said, "What is this thing that thou doest to the people"? Why sittest thou thyself alone, and all the people stand by thee from morning unto even? And Moses said unto his father-in-law, Because the people come unto me to inquire of God: when they have a matter, they come unto me; and I judge between one and another, and I do make them know the statutes of God, and His laws". Therefore Moses was teaching them. He said that he was. All right, "And Moses' father-in-law said unto him, The thing that thou doest is not good. Thou wilt surely wear away, both you, and this people that is with thee, for this thing is too heavy for thee; thou art not able to perform it thyself alone. Hearken now unto my voice, I will give thee council, and God shall be with thee: Be thou for the people to Godward, that thou mayest bring the causes unto God: and thou shalt teach them ordinances and laws, and shalt show them the way wherein they must walk, and the work that they must do. Moreover thou shalt provide out of all the people able men, such as fear God, men of truth, hating covetousness; and place such over them, to be rulers over thousands, and rulers of hundreds, rulers of fifties, and rulers of tens; and let them judge the people at all seasons; and it shall be, that every great matter they shall bring unto thee, but every small matter they shall judge; so shall it be easier for thyself, and they shall bear the burden with thee. If thou shalt do this thing, and God command thee so, then thou shalt be able to endure, and all this people shall also go all to their place in peace. So Moses hearkened to the voice of his father-in-law, and did all that he had said. And Moses chose able men out of all Israel, and made them heads over the people, rulers of thousands, rulers of hundreds, rulers of fifties, and rulers of tens. And they judged the people at all seasons; the hard causes they brought unto Moses, but every small matter they judged themselves. Now, I want you to notice that arrangement. Moses, according to the suggestion of his father-in-law, placed rulers over thousands, rulers over hundreds, rulers over fifties, and rulers over tens. For what purpose? To keep from wearing himself out and wearing the people out. They were all coming to Moses and had to sit and wait there turn, and it took so long for Moses to get to them, he had to sit there from morning until evening. And so it wore him out, and it wore the people out; and his father-in-law suggested this method of arrangement, and Moses did it, and the arrangement was carried out. What do we find? (Chart no. 2) Well, in Numbers 1:46 we learn that among Israel those who were numbered from twenty years old and upward among the men able to go to war, there were 603,550. That is to say nothing about all the women and all the others. But here we have 603,550. Now, then, if a ruler or a teacher was placed over the thousands, there would be 603 teachers. And then if there was a ruler placed over the hundreds, there would be 6,035 teachers among them. Then if there were teachers or judges placed over the fifties there would be 12,071. And rulers placed over the tens, or judges placed over the tens, there would be 60,355. Therefore, this arrangement suggested by the father-in-law of Moses and put into effect by Moses required 79,064 teachers teaching the word of God to Israel during that time. I insist that they could not all have done it consecutively; because had it been done consecutively, one after another, the people would have been just as much worn cut waiting for the next man as they would have if they had waited for Moses in the first place. And, consequently, this requires that there be *simultaneous teaching*. There had to be simultaneous teaching. This system could not operate, it was utterly impossible for it to operate, without simultaneous teaching. Now, then, I suggest that if the command to teach in the Old Testament could be made to include an arrangement of this kind, then why cannot the commandment to teach in the New Testament involve such an arrangement as our classes? What's the difference?

Well, I pass on again. The next argument I want to base upon a statement made in the fifth chapter of Acts of the Apostles. I turn and read this. I know what it says, but I want to read it. Here men were placed in prison. The apostles were thrown into prison because they were teaching the truth, and they were to be brought before the Council the next day; but when the angels came and delivered them, and the men were sent for them the next morning, they were gone. They were not there, and they came back and reported that the men were missing. They were not there, and they had been told by the angel to "go stand and speak in the the temple to the people all the words of this life". And while they were discussing this matter, finding that the men were missing, we are told in verse 25, "Then came one and told them, Behold, the men whom ye put in prison are standing in the temple, and teaching the people". Now, I want you to notice that. "The men are standing and teaching the people". Now, then, if it had said *the men stood and taught the people,* we wouldn't know anything about when it was done. It might be one man stood one day, another man another day; one man one year, another man another year, if it had just said *the men stood.* But the report says the "men *are standing* (present tense); *"the men are standing in the temple".* "The men (plural number) are standing (present tense) and teaching the people (present tense)." Therefore, we have a plural number of men engaged in teaching in the present tense. "The men are standing and teaching", and there's simultaneous teaching found in this book of the Acts of the apostles'.

Then I pass to this fact: that oftentimes Jesus Christ followed this principle, that he took one group out of another group and taught it. First, I call your attention to a statement in the seventh chapter of Mark. Much oftentimes has been said by these brethren about assemblies being called. There must be a *called assembly* for it to constitute an assembly such as they require. In the seventh chapter of Mark, beginning with verse 14 we read, "And when *he had called all the people unto him".* There is a called assembly. Jesus called them. When he had called all the people unto him, he said unto them, "Hearken unto me, everyone of you, and understand; there is nothing from without a man, that entering into him can defile him: but the things which came out of him, those are that which defile the man. If any man have ears to hear, let him hear." There the Lord called the multitude together. He called the people to him. It was a called assembly, called by Jesus Christ himself. And then the Lord taught that assembly that he had called to him. Then in verse 17 we are told that "when he was entered in the house *from the people,* his disciples asked him concerning the parable". All right, he called the assembly together, and he taught the whole assembly. Then he *divided the assembly.* He took some of them away from that assembly into another place and taught them, and there he explained to his disciples about some matters along the line, from verse 17 on down through verse 23. So Jesus called an assembly; He taught that assembly; then he divided that assembly and took some of them away and taught the ones that he took away. Certainly that's the very principle upon which we operate. I'm not claiming in all these cases there are parallels in every point. My opponent has already admitted last night that things may be parallel in one point but not parallel in some other. And the parallel I'm claiming for this is that the assembly was divided, and, furthermore, that the group that was taken away was taught. One group taken away from another group, and that group taken away was taught by Jesus Christ, the Son of God.

And not only that, but I call your attention again to a statement regarding the trip one time on their way to Jerusalem. In Luke 13:31-33 we are told that Jesus "took unto him the twelve". There was the multitude. Jesus took the twelve away from them. Jesus took unto him the twelve and he began to explain to them that he was going to Jerusalem, there to be rejected and crucified and be raised against the third day. And then Matthew records the same incident in Matt. 20:17-19. He took the twelve apart, by themselves, Matthew says, and this is not the only time the Lord ever followed that course, for in Mark 10:32-34, Mary says: "He took again the twelve." He had done it before. He does *again.* So the Lord had followed that course on different occasions of talking one group away from another group and teaching the group that he took away. Thus we have another parallel with respect to taking a group away from a larger group and teaching the group that was taken away. We have authority, therefore, in the practice of Jesus Christ, from the principles involved in those statements, to do that very thing which we are doing when we take one group away from another group and teach the group that we take away.

But then there is another point I want to get, in connection with that, at the transfiguration. I am going at this time to Mark, the ninth chapter. You'll find the transfiguration recorded in different parts, or course, of the Gospel writings; but in the ninth chapter of Mark I want to notice here another incident. In verse 2 we are told, "And after six days Jesus taketh with him Peter, James and John, and leadeth them up into a high mountain apart by themselves." Now, he took them away from all the rest of the multitude, even from all the rest of the disciples. Three men he took away from all the rest, bringing them up into a high mountain apart by themselves, and he was transfigured before them. There Moses and Elijah appeared talking to him, and the voice of God spoke and told them, "This is my beloved Son in whom I am well pleased: hear ye Him". Even the God of Heaven on that occasion taught the group that was taken away. Not only so, but we find in Mark 9:9-13 and also Luke 9:37 that when they came down from the mountain on the next day, there was teaching still going on. The Lord was teaching them regarding the statement concerning the Elijah which was to come. They were engaged in that sort of teaching, and they made the approach back to the place where the other disciples were, and verse 14 says, "And when he came to his disciples, he saw a great multitude about them, and the Scribes questioning with them." Not questioning them, but *questioning with them;* and the Revised Standard Version, which Brother Abercrombie introduced the other night, says, *"arguing with them"*. So there were teaching — there was instruction going on in the group that was left behind. There was simultaneous teaching — the Lord teaching in the group as they came down from the mountain, and there was the other group of the disciples out there teaching the multitude at the same time. Engaged in the discussion — engaged in argument about things divine, about those things involved upon that occasion. And so there we have a parallel of our simultaneous teaching. I have shown you the parallels in the practice of Jesus Christ: that he *called an assembly,* that he *divided the assembly,* that he *took groups away from larger groups* and taught the groups that he took away. Furthermore, I have shown you that teaching was done in the group that was left behind. So we have simultaneous teaching as well as the teaching otherwise mentioned here. Thank you, Ladies and Gentlemen.

Abercrombie's First Speech
Third Night — December 6, 1951 (Negative)

Ladies and Gentlemen, worthy opponent:

I am indeed happy to be here tonight to deny the proposition which has just been affirmed in this discussion. I wholeheartedly concur with the moderator that we are here in search of truth. We shall endeavor tonight to set forth the truth as it is revealed in the precious word of God.

The last two nights I proved by the precious word of God that it is sinful to divided the church up into a plurality of classes for simultaneous teaching with women teaching some of those classes. We showed that to be true from I Cor. 14:31 where Paul commanded them to speak one by one to all that all may learn and all may be comforted, and forbid women to speak in any assembly of the church — verses 33, 34, and 35, "It is a shame for women to speak in the church". Brother Porter has agreed and has admitted that the church — the Sunday School — *is the church*. That is the distinction which he made between missionary society and the Sunday School. It is the church assembly. *It is an assembly of the church.*

We are here tonight to continue this investigation and I am happy to stand before you in defense of the truth of the Almighty God. Arranging into classes, women may teach some of these classes; now, that's what my brother is here trying to find. He must find a church of Jesus Christ practicing what he has affirmed in his proposition. He is seeking a New Testament Chruch of Christ practicing simultaneous teaching with women teaching some of those classes. I am going to hold him to the issue and I am going to keep this issue before the people of what he is trying to prove. He would try to get your mind away from the issue on something else or way back to Moses or sometime back there, when the Church wasn't established until A.D. 33 in the city of Jerusalem. He will try to take some practice back then. He doesn't endorse the things they did there.

But we'll take that up in just a few moments and we'll see that he won't stand with it. His position is untenable. Says "authorized" — that means that it's in harmony with scriptural principles. I Cor. 14:31 shows that his classifying of the church is not in harmony with scriptural principle.

He mentions the Kerrville School. My knowledge and understanding of that is that they teach one by one unto all. Now, I don't know as to the doctrinal soundness of everything taught there. I have never been there, and have never met Brother Shelburne. I wouldn't vouch for that. As to the order they had advertised that it's being taught by one man speaking at a time and that's what the advertisements say. And he tries to make it appear that they have something out there that is unscriptural. It's no more unscriptural than speaking to this audience tonight, as far as the order is concerned.

He mentions the Church Messenger and brought up Brother Dennis Kellog. And incidentally, Brother Dennis Kellog is the author of a little tract that this congregation and others are circulating around here. And it might be surprising to you to know that Brother Dennis Kellog says that the parents of children seven and eight years old may go into the class, this class, that's taught by these women. Yes sir, he believes that women can teach the parents of the children, can go in and sit in the class where the women is teaching these children. Brother Porter won't have it. No sir.

(Moderator, Brother J. A. Dennis: "Emphasize that men can go into her classes.")

Yes, sir, the parents — of course that would include the man. And so therefore they can go into the classes and there we see that he is crossed.

Now then, we notice something else. He mentioned seven preachers, seven preachers that had left us and had gone over to them, and he wanted me to mention some that had left them and come over to us. Would that prove his practice? Friends, there is a man that left them (Pointing to Brother J. A. Dennis). Paul Knight left them. Leland Knight left them, Brother Moore left them in Alabama and we could just add to that list and infinitum, just go on and on, showing that they have left them and come to us. Ah, he couldn't make anything out of that!

The Tingley Debate. Porter said, "the scriptures teach" — I used that to show how Porter kicked and bucked when a man tried to bring in extraneous and irrelevant matter into the proposition that they were discussing. And that's what he has been doing for two nights, and I showed him that that's the way he reacted. And of course he tried to patch that up tonight but he couldn't patch it.

One group with one teacher. Oh yes! We had that just ready to use but our time played out. Simultaneous teaching, one speaking at a time — You know, he tried to parallel this multitude of people, some 400 they say the first night — he tried to parallel this multitude of people to his simultaneous class teaching. How many were speaking at a time? I am amazed and everybody else should be. The very idea! Jesus taught multitudes. He talked about some, maybe being back there and some over yonder in that corner. Well, here's some right here divided from those right over there, Brother Porter. But we don't have but one assembly and one teacher and that's the principle of the Lord which is outlined. Let's notice that a little more. Notice furthermore that it was not parallel with his Sunday School because there were no women teaching in this assembly.

By the way, Brother Porter, would it be scriptural for women to teach the people who were in the basement the other night? If it is parallel with your Sunday School? Then according to you they could teach — the women could teach — the group in the basement or back there. That shows you what trouble he gets in. Everything he uses reacts unfavorable on his position. He tried to have a little fun on that but it backfired. Porter says on I Cor. 14:31, Porter said, yes, "Speak one by one to one assembly". "Yes, that's what the apostle said." That's what the Lord authorized. But he didn't authorize his plurality of assemblies out of that one; tearing it up into various segregations, parts, and put women over part of that church assembly. That's the thing that he can't prove. If I didn't misunderstand him he said, "I don't believe in more than one speaking to one group." Now that's when he was making this argument about this assembly the other night, "I don't believe in one speaking to more than one group." After this he charged me with speaking to more than one group by speaking to the same audience that he was speaking to. He was doing the same thing that he charged me with doing. "Didn't believe in it." He ought to quit it. I'm speaking to a multitude. All of that was just some more of his "consistency"!! Irrelevancy — impertinent matter, pertains not to the proposition. It is not parallel whatsoever!

Porter said, "You would think that all that we do is class teaching." We came here to discuss class teaching — that's why we are talking about class teaching. He wants to talk about everything else. He wants you to forget that we are here to discuss class teaching. That's what I'm here for. That's where we disagree. That's where we are divided. We're trying to get the brethren together on this thing and get them to lay aside the doctrines and commandments of men and unite on the truth that there be no division among us. "We can teach the whole group in one assembly", Brother Porter said. Yes, we can teach it and therefore his classifying — all that is not necessary. He has admitted he didn't have to do that. Well, Paul did it without classifying and commanded it to be done without classifying in I Cor. 14:31. Why substitute man's ways for God's way? God's manner or way of edifying the church and doing away with confusion is for the men to speak one by one to all that all may learn and all may be comforted. Now, that's God's plan. Oh, they say, "Well we're going to do it otherwise." "We'll build classrooms and we'll have them to all talk at once." Some of his other brethren, catch onto it. They say, "Well now, we want to do just like you brethren are doing, but we don't have money to build classrooms. We have a very small auditorium, and so what are we going to do, Brother Porter?" What does this Brother do about such cases as that? Oh, he said, "I would recommend that they not do that if it cause confusion." But they do practice classifying where they have small auditoriums and more than one speaker speaking at a time and they have women speaking in the presence of men, and can be heard by men. And he says that's wrong and sinful. *Are they going to hell for it?* If they are you ought to convert them. Oh, how he retreated last night! He asked for all that stuff I was putting out on him and he began to retreat and, "Oh, I don't believe in that." "No, I don't endorse that." "I find that just as bad as you do" "Oh, I hate that." Oh, yes! He just began to go in circles last night. *Talking about "must" — Porter said those men must speak like Paul said in that assembly; and when he said that, it ruined his classifying because that was the teaching service that the Lord authorized and it forbids classifying — "speak one by one" — Porter has them all talking at once.* There Paul had them in an undivided assembly and taught by men speaking one at a time. Porter has them in many different grades and groups and has a plurality of teachers and women teachers — and Paul says that is a "shame". "I suffer not a woman to teach". That's where he's talking about teaching — in assemblies of the church.

Can you find a passage that says you must not use instruments of music? Just one verse, please. You know how he cut-up on that! Just show one verse that says in so many words — that's what he meant. "Thou must not divide into classes." I asked him to give one verse that, "Thou must not use mechanical instruments of music to accompany singing." Has he produced it? No, he didn't produce it. He is using secretarian logic (?). A digressive argument, that that what is not expressly condemned is allowed. This will justify a mourner's bench, sprinkling of babies, turnip greens on the Lord's table, and any other thing that men wanted to bring in. That's the kind of logic or sophistry he tried to pull over me. I Cor. 14:31 is a divine law. Can Porter put a verse on the board that says what I just required or asked of him? He cannot. He can find where it says "sing", but he won't find that other. I showed how God commanded teaching to be done, and for women to be silent in such assemblies. He can't find anything that resembles his practice. He can find where they had singing. Where is the scripture that says you must not use or put turnip greens on the Lord's table? He repudiates much of the Sunday School practices, and we have hopes that he will have great success in converting them, when he's converted — that he'll convert his brethren. We're hoping for that.

The Sunday School is an institution to *do* teaching. It is the church made into something that the New Testament does not teach and, expressly forbids. At Taft Brother Porter said there wasn't a singing school in the Bible. I showed it to him for his benefit and that the people might know Porter didn't know what he was talking about. Last night he tried to slip out by saying I couldn't find the "name" in the Bible. I hope they publish that debate and this one also, and then the record will show what was said and what wasn't. Last night Brother Porter beat a retreat from what his brethren are doing. And yet he's trying to tack some things probably that my brethren are doing on me; and some of the things he charged I know absolutely are not true concerning my brethren having simultaneous teaching — classifying the church. They are not doing that. He insisted that such be brought into this debate; so now he has it. He condemns certain things that have come out of the Sunday School. I hope that he will certainly be converted and convert them. (How much time? Thank you.)

Now then, to the teaching service. Mentioned Brother

Leland Knight — who has been teaching in Oklahoma City. Brother Leland Knight teaches there — in general church assembly. Brother Knight, incidentally, was one of the preachers who left the Sunday School faction and came over to preach the truth. Porter, said he wasn't drifting last night. He's not drifting! I agree with him. He's landed in secretarianism. "Women can preach over the radio if they will not preach to men — if men won't listen." Try to tune them out! But listen, he has established a new order of evangelists. Now that's what Sunday Schoolism is doing — that's why his position is untenable. A new order of evangelists — women evangelists. *Hold evangelistic meetings for women only.* What would be the difference in this, Brother Porter, and preaching over a radio if only men listened? What about that? Now, then, women can go out in the sap oaks in the thickets and set up a tent or a brush arbor and invite all the women in the country and preach to them. Can she baptize?

Now, they had an all women church at Montevallo when I met Brother Garrett in debate. Brother Porter said that I didn't know what I was talking about there. Well, I try to know what I am talking about. I might miss it sometime. But I incidentally went to Montevallo and I talked to the Sister Evangelist, the leader of that church, and she told me herself, that when men didn't come she conducted the services herself. I talked to them over at the college and they said that people weren't forbidden to come. Six miles from a church of Christ — I presume they have men running it! And a Greyhound bus running right beside that Montevallo church to Calera every day. You know how Brother Garrett tried to patch that up? Oh, he said they probably haven't got enough money to ride the bus up there. Haven't got enough money — going to college — haven't got bus fare. It would be better to walk than to do something forbidden by the precious word of God. Walk six miles. "In search of truth — arranging into classes." I'll see how much of this junk I've covered.

Now then we come to Matt. 28:19 and he argued about "go". Walk, swim, skate, ride. He's on skates. He was skating last night, but he wasn't on his feet! We agree that "go" is generic and I showed these people that he has already abandoned his position. Why, he has admitted in this discussion that teach — that it is not as generic as "go". Oh, he has put many "musts" on that word "teach". *He found the "must" in*

I Cor. 14:31. And he can find just a lot of other *musts* over there in I Cor. 14. He found some restrictions over there and so have I. And so all this just goes for hot air. I baptize in water. He walked about a pool, a baptistry, and a lake, and a river. They baptized no doubt in lakes, rivers. What does that have to do with the propositon here tonight? Not one thing. Talking about singing, we're agreed on singing, we are not divided over that.

Now then we come down here, and we notice "teach". He mentions a pulpit. He mentions printing presses, radio, chart, and he groups with that classes. Now, then we're going to notice a few things. Classes are not parallel with these things, for the simple reason that they are not in harmony with I Cor. 14:31-35. They violate those principles. I Tim. 2:11-12, Paul says, "I suffer not a woman to teach nor usurp authority over the man, but to be in silence." Those principles are violated in class teaching. Furthermore, concerning pulpits, printing presses, radio preaching, preaching over the radio, charts, he knows that the use we make of such expedients is in harmony with the scriptures. We agree. Porter and I agree on that, the use that I make of it. He does not charge me with sinning in standing on a pulpit, using a printing press or preaching over the radio or writing on a piece of paper the scriptures or using a chart or blackboard. Now then, all of these things could be made sinful or violate principles of truth. The pulpit could be used wrongly. Most of them are — to preach false doctrine upon. Printing press — they are used wrongly and print lots of things that are wrong. The radio — Brother Porter admitted that it could be used wrong. Let a woman get on there and preach — and let men listen in. A chart could be used wrongly. But classes, violate the scriptures, and the use that I make of these expediences are in harmony with the scriptures, and he cannot and does not and dare not charge that the use I make of them are sinful. But classes are not parallel, they do not fall in that category they do not belong there, and that scripture right there will get them out. I Peter 4:11 — "If any man speak let him speak as the oracles of God. God's oracles do not allow what he practices. That's where I stand and he cannot move it. A veritable Gibralter has "squshed' him. "Play organ, harp, banjo, violin." All right. He says that this is not parallel. We'll give him a parallel. Let us notice this now. "Go, *play* on instruments and sing." "Go *divide* into classes and teach." *Two additions.* One of them is *"play" on instruments* and sing; the other is, *the other addition, "Divide" into classes* and teach. *Dividing into classes is just as different from teaching as playing is from singing.* There's your parallel. *Two additions — added to the word of God.* He belongs to the Christian Church but won't admit it! That's where he ought to go. If I could swallow what he's trying to palm off on you good people, I'd carry along something to make music too. The way he brings in that would bring in musical instruments. So the Sunday School is not parallel? It violates the word of God. Mark 16:15, Go preach the gospel". We're agreed on that — that statement, if they do it upon God's word. If they obey this they will do away with the Sunday School. He said nothing about classes as far as the word is concerned. Well, we'll pass that for the moment.

Porter is hunting simultaneous teaching when the church assembles with women teachers. Women teaching. (How much time? About 8 minutes. Thank you. Wish I had forty.)

Now then we have shown that Sunday Schools and instruments of music are on a par. They belong together. They have as their sole foundation the doctrines and commandments of men. "Classes — a means of doing what God commanded". They are a means of disobeying God's word. If he'd said that he would have been right. Where did the church employ this? It violates the scriptures which I have read. Now then, we wish to notice all of this that we possibly can. yes, now then we'll come to another part of the things that he said.

Concerning Deuteronomy 6 — Israel was to teach. Exodus 18:13, Moses had a burden that was too heavy for him. And so we find that he parallels this with Sunday School simultaneous teaching when the church assembles. Now that's proof, isn't it? Moses had a big job; the burden was too heavy for him, and it concerned *all Israel.* That gets all the tribes of Israel just like it would include for this Nation all the States of the United States. All right. He tried to parallel that with his Sunday School. The burden was too heavy for Moses so they selected men, faithful or able men. *Did they put any women in there?* Your proposition calls for women in some of those classes. All right. No women were there, so there is no parallel there. But now then we notice just a little more about this. What was the reason for this great division over *all Israel?* Had too many for Moses to take care of. That's the reason. Now is the Sunday

School organized for his purpose? Now, see if it's paralled there. Do they organize the Sunday School because they have too many people for the preacher to teach?

Here's something from Brother Emmons in Birmingham. He says in the church bulletin at Central Church, "We have in mind such as Bible School, prayer meeting, Sunday evening worship service, *Bible classes*. Only a very small percent of the members usually attend these meetings. If visitors did not come out our way it would really look pitiful on occasions." That's parallel there, isn't it? Moses, because he had too many divided up *all Israel* but they do not do it for that reason. "It looked pitiful on occasions", Brother Emmons said. So they — he doesn't have to have assistant teachers because the burden is too heavy. But now then Col. 2:14 "Blotting out the handwriting of ordinances which was against us, which was contrary to us, taking it out of the way and nailing it to his cross."

John 1:17 — "The law was given by Moses but grace and truth came by Jesus Christ." If he could find a replica of his Sunday School in every iota of similarity it would go for no proof today since, my friends, we are under the *law of Jesus Christ*. And the very thing that he seeks to substantiate, its underlying principles violate the teaching of the Lord and puts women plainly in violation of God's injunction in which he says women are not to teach in assemblies of the church. *And Porter applied I Cor. 14:31 to classes; and, friends, verse 35 goes in with it*. "It is a shame for women to speak in church." So that will do for that for the present.

"Acts", we'll have to get to, I see, "the transfiguration", I believe, in the next speech. Let us take up Acts 5:25 at this time. Now then, let us notice — "The men whom ye put in prison are now standing in the temple and teaching the people." If I gave it correctly. Now then he takes that to mean that they "*must*" all be speaking at the same time. Now that's the interpretation he puts on that. Don't forget it. He's got a *must* there. Just as much *must* there as he charged me of having and yet he admitted the must was in the scripture that I offered I Cor. 14:31. But now then, friends, they must — in order to have simultaneous teaching — they must all be speaking at the same time, *don't forget it*. All right, he takes it that where the plural pronoun is used in the present tense, it therefore must mean a plurality of speakers are speaking at the same time. And he assumes — he reads between the lines — that it

—114—

was classified. All right, just one example for the present which will upset him completely. Acts 2:6-7 — "Now when this was noised abroad the multitude came together and were confounded because that every man heard them speak" — Is that the present tense? — "heard them *speak* in his own language." Well, let's notice the seventh verse and see what it says. "And they were all amazed and marvelled saying one to another, "Behold, are not all these which speak" — I know that's present tense, I know — "Are not all these which speak Galileans". All right, what has he made? From his supposition and his illogical interpretation of the scripture and even grammatical usage he now has one multitude — *they came together* — being taught simultaneously by twelve men all speaking at the same time. *If it teaches that, in Acts 5:25 it teaches that here.* We find that when a group of people authorize one man to speak for them and they concur with his remarks it is gramatical in anyone's rhetoric, to say "they spake" when only one man was speaking for them. We have many examples to prove that. Now then, we shall notice another scripture — Luke 24:19-36, we have a parallel. (How much time? We hope to have time later. Is the time up?) I thank you kindly for listening.

Porter's Second Affirmative Speech
Third Night — December 6, 1951

Brother Abercrombie, Ladies and Gentlemen:

If I ever in my life say a poor boy that needed some time, I saw him a while. ago. For if any man ever needed time, Cecil needed it a while ago, as anyone in the audience can readily see.

I want to take up the speech that he made and give my attention to the things that he said. He began by saying that "I proved last night that it was sinful to divide into groups to teach, and I proved it by I Cor. 14:31." Well, it just so happens that *he didn't prove any such thing*. I Cor. 14:31 doesn't say one single, solitary word about remaining in one group or remaining in undivided assemblies. It doesn't say it; *it just isn't there*. Cecil just reads it into it. It's not there, and Cecil knows it's not there, and all of his brethren know it isn't there, and they have known it all of these years; and they can't find it, and *they know that they can't find it*. Here he gets up here and makes a bald assertion that "I proved so-and-so", *when he proved nothing of the sort*. And if he did, then he proved that Jesus Christ committed a sin, for I showed you tonight that Jesus Christ called a multitude together — he called an assembly — that he taught that assembly, and then he took a group away from that assembly, and he taught the group that he took away. And if he proved that it was sinful, then he proved that Jesus Christ did sin, and therefore was a sinful man. He proved too much by I Cor. 14:31.

"In order for Porter to sustain his proposition he must find," he says, "a New Testament church practicing simultaneous teaching with women teachers in some of their classes." In other words, I must find the thing specifically stated that they arranged into classes in order for it to be scriptural at all. Well, I could very easily turn the thing around, and the other brethren do turn it on him when he gets in a debate. In order for him to prove, according to his own argument, that he is scriptural in his contention for a plurality of cups in communion, he must find some New Testament church practicing a plurality of cups. And did not those "one-cup" brethren you met in debate call upon you for something like that? And did you give it? He must find a New Testament church practicing that. Now, the fact is, I get the classes for teaching exactly like he gets the plurality of cups for the communion. Exactly the same! And if I must find a New Testament church practicing dividing into classes, to find in scriptural authority for classes, then he must find one practicing plurality of cups in communion to find any authority for that. And he must find one practicing plurality of cups in communion to find any authority for that. And he must find a New Testament church using song books in their worship in order to have any authority for his use of song books. Can he find it? No. I get the classes by the same process that he gets the song books, and in order for him to prove his contention about singing schools, he must find a New Testament church practicing the operation of singing schools. Can he find it? No, and yet he thinks it's perfectly scriptural. Why, then, must I find one practicing classes to be scriptural when he can be scriptural on all these other points without finding the New Testament church practicing them? That's the inconsistency of anti-Bible class advocates.

Regarding the Kerrville School, he said, "Now, they teach one by one, and Porter tried to prove that it was unscriptural." *Porter didn't try to do any such thing.* I believe those brethren are doing scriptural work. I didn't try to prove that it was unscriptural. I just said that you brethren were trying to do the very thing that you brethren condemn, that's all. And they're operating a Bible School. They're having groups come there and teach in the groups. Oh, he said, "Well, now, after all it doesn't make any difference." They have groups — they have one group for this and another group for that later, and still another group; and so there are groups being taught. But Cecil says, "You can't teach groups; you've got to have the whole thing together at the same time."

Regarding Dennis Kellog who gave up the anti-class advocacy and took his stand with us, he said that Kellog says the parents of children may go to the classes. Well, suppose he does. That doesn't prove he didn't leave you, does it? And regardless of what he may say about it, does that prove that he didn't leave you fellows? I simply gave proof that he left. He's one of the preachers that left you fellows, regardless of what he says. So that didn't help you any. Oh, but he was going to give me a bunch of them that left us, and whom did he give? Such fellows as Paul Knight and Leland Knight, that dates away back yonder years ago, and some of the fellows that helped put the thing over that he's advocating tonight; some of those

fellows away back there that helped put this thing into operation almost — way back yonder, years ago — these men were. I
thought the way he talked last night that a whole bunch of my
brethren left me last week maybe and joined hands with him.

In the Tingley debate, "Porter was raving because Tingley
was bringing extraneous matters." Well, of course, Cecil
doesn't do that; he harps about the Missionary Society, instrumental music, and mourners' benches, and sprinkling, and
turnip greens on the Lord's table, but he doesn't bring in extraneous matters. Don't you see?

And then one group with one teacher — this assembly.
Regarding this assembly, he said, "Now, Porter's been asking
about this assembly that's been here during this debate — if I
could scripturally teach this assembly." Why, he said, "That
thing backfired on Porter because we are not having
simultaneous teaching." Well, that's the thing I expected you
to say, Cecil — exactly. But your proposition said *more than
simultaneous teaching* — Your proposition the past two nights
said that when people come together to be taught by the
church, first, "they must remain in one group", AND "they
must be taught by men only, speaking one at a time". There
were two parts of this proposition. Are you going to give up
one of them? The first part said *they must remain in one group;*
the second part said *they must be taught by men only.* Cecil
says I'm willing to surrender the first part if you'll just let me
keep the rest of it. "Yes, let me keep the last part, I'll give up
the first part of it," because he's guilty, you see. He's doing the
very thing that his proposition said couldn't be done, because
he's been speaking to more than one group, during this debate,
in various rooms of this building, even some down in the basement. *Yes, he has.* And his proposition said: First, "they must
remain in one group," AND "be taught by men only, one
speaking at a time." So there are two parts to this proposition.
He's giving up one of them *by his practice;* and now he's just
about tried to surrender it *by his speech* in order to hold the
rest of it. Thank you, Cecil.

Then, when the congregation, when the people come
together for the purpose of teaching, they *don't have to remain
in one group.* Do they? It is not sinful to remain in different
groups. That is not the sin then. So the sin doesn't come in
separating the groups. *The separation is not the sin,* according
to Cecil, because he has been doing that very thing for three

nights. Well, the backfire backfired. he wants to know if it is scriptural for women to teach those in the basement. I don't know who are in the basement, and therefore I couldn't answer his question unless I knew who were in the basement.

All right, I Cor. 14:31. He says *you must not tear up the assembly.* On I Cor. 14:31 he says you must not tear up the assembly. He tore this one up. You must not tear up the assembly. All right, they come together in the assembly — we must not tear it up. Then, Cecil, I want you to answer this: Suppose, Cecil, that those who have part in the Bible class teaching do not come together in an assembly like this, but each class goes direct to its own place of teaching. You won't tear up any assembly then. *Can that be done?* Suppose we don't have an assembly beforehand to tear up, and let each group go to its own class room. *Could two groups or three groups from the same congregation go to three parts of East Point and have simultaneous teaching?* Could a group of men meet here for special training? Can another group meet further south in town? And another group further west in town somewhere? If they didn't come together first, but each group went direct to it's place, could they do that, Cecil? Now, you tell me — you are wanting to be fair. You're wanting to answer questions. You wanted to get this thing above board. So come right on now.

Let's see about this: "Porter admits that he can teach in one group, and, therefore, his classes are not necessary. And since he admits that he can teach on one group, then quit your class teaching." Well, Cecil admits that he can preach in a pulpit and not over a radio; then, why don't you quit your radio preaching? You admit that you can teach without it — so why go to a radio station?

Concerning the matter of eliminating confusion, he said, "They try to eliminate confusion by building class rooms, and sometimes they have classes in the same room." And he says, "They try to eliminate the confusion by building class rooms, but the Lord's way to eliminate confusion is for one to speak at a time." No, the class rooms don't eliminate that confusion that the Lord talked about, because you can separate into a dozen class rooms and still have the same confusion that Paul talked about in I Cor. 14:31. You can have a dozen different classes in a dozen different rooms and have two persons speaking at the same time to each class and have the very same confusion that they had in the auditorium to begin with. The class, the walls of the class rooms, serves the same purpose that six blocks would serve between me and another congregation over there. Yet we can have the same confusion in both classes that Paul referred to. You will have to try it over, Cecil.

He talked about Porter retracting last night, "Oh, he retracted and got very emotional about it." Yes, sir, "I don't endorse this; I brought that up," I "don't endorse this." and I "went around in circles." Well, I admit that I did. I was following Cecil. Cecil was in the affirmative. I was just following him. Why, certainly I went in circles, I wouldn't follow in the negative without going in circles. That's why I went around in circles.

But he wants me to produce one verse that says *you must not use an instrument,* and Porter is getting "the old sectarian argument that whatever is not specifically prohibited is accepted." I've never made an argument like that. Nothing I've said last night nor tonight *even indicated such a thing.* But he said, "Now show me one verse that says you *must not use an instrument.*" He said last night *that his law said you must.* He said God made that law. You know when I said that Cecil made the law, *that God didn't make it,* he came right back and said, "God put the *must* in there — that *God is the one that made the law and said you must do it.*" Well, if God said "you must do it," tell me when he said it. That's what I wanted; not "must not", but "must". Must is the thing I'm talking about; not must not, but *Must.* You said it *must* be done.

Now, he says, "I'll tell you what I can find. I can find where it says "sing"." So can I. Now, you find where it says "remain" Yes, sir, you don't have to find where it says *you must not* divided into classes. Just find where it says "remain", and you will have it, just like if it said "play", you would have instrumental music". I can find where it says "sing"; therefore, I don't have to find where it says you "must not" use the instrument. Now the thing for him to do is to find where it says "remain'. Remain! And that is what he hasn't found.

"Sunday School", he says, "is an institution." "In the Taft debate, Porter said there wasn't any such thing in the Bible as a singing school, and I gave him 1 Chron. 25:7-9". It wouldn't be necessary to reply to that tonight except that some may be here tonight that were not here last night. The fact is I called upon Cecil, produce an example of his singing school, and he gave me 1 Chron. 25:7-9. That was the example of *his* singing school. We were discussing the singing school like he and his brethren were teaching, but he gave me that, and I turned to the verse preceding the one which he read and showed they had cymbals, psalteries, and harps in it. And so I turned him over to the Christian Church. That's where he belonged, according to that argument. I wouldn't need to mention that tonight again except for the fact that some of you were not here last night.

Oh, he hopes they will publish that debate and this one, too. Why don't you publish one of them, Cecil? Now, you know these fellows have done a lot of crowing about the Taft debate never being printed. It never was recorded for the purpose of being printed that I ever heard of. Brethren recorded it that they might take it home with them and play it to the people that couldn't come and hear it. But these brethren began to harp through their papers that here's a debate that will never be printed, and they kept on pushing that, and finally I wrote Cecil and said, "If you know somebody that can print it, I will cooperate with you a hundred per cent". Cecil lost interest. It takes money to publish debates. Well, Cecil, why didn't you publish?

(Bro. Abercrombie speaks from his seat: "I didn't have the money".)

Well, all right then, somebody else might be in the same shape.

"Porter is not drifting. He has already landed in sectarianism." And that's what Ervin Waters says Cecil has done on the cup question. Yes, he says, "He is not drifting; he has already landed in sectaranism with his plurality of cups for the communion service." Every time he makes a stab like that it just boomerangs right back on his own head.

He returned to the "all-woman church at Montevallo." He talked with a Sister Evangelist Hood, he said, and she said that she conducted the service herself when no man was there. Well, all the details of that I do not now. I do know that a brother told me that he had no knowledge of ever a time being when some brother, some man, was not there to conduct the worship service, but let that be as it may.

I want to ask Cecil this question: If three women member of the church, Cecil, riding in an airplane, crossing some foreign country, were forced to land at some place 5,000 miles away from a church, and those women were forced to stay there for a long period of time, could they worship God? Come on now and answer that. *Could those three women worship if they landed 5,000 miles away from any church, and there were no means to get out maybe for months?* Could those women worship God during that time? Tell me.

This blackboard chart he dismissed with "hot air" and the wave of his hand, with the exception of very little of it. He says that's all hot air — goodbye! And very little he said about it. I'm going to pay attention to what little he did say. He said the classes are not parallel with these others because the classes violate 1 Cor. 14:31. Classes do not violate 1 Cor. 14:31. 1 Cor. 14:31 regulates one teacher for one assembly, one teacher for one group, and in classes we never have but one teacher for one group. There's no violation. Has Cecil ever said anything about that? Not one single, solitary word, though I have pressed that in every speech of this debate. He has never mentioned it any more than just to wave his hand at it and say "goodbye". That's the way he deals with it. *Come on, Cecil and tell me something about it.*

But he knows the use of radios is scriptural. He doesn't charge me with saying that Cecil said it. Why, certainly I know it is scriptural. But I know that you get it exactly on the same basis that I got the classes; and, therefore, I know that the classes are scriptural upon the same basis that we both know that the radio is scriptural.

But he says that some of those thing could be wrong. "You take the pulpit," he said, "the pulpit could be wrong. There might be false doctrine preached from it. and the printing press could be wrong. There might be false doctrine printed, and the radio could be wrong. There might be false doctrine proclaimed over it. And the chart could be wrong. There might be false doctrine proclaimed in it. And on the same basis I admit that the classes could be wrong. But that doesn't make the pulpit wrong does it? No! It's what is done. It is the teaching that is done that is wrong — not the pulpit. The pulpit is not wrong because some man teaches false doctrine. It is the thing that he teaches that is wrong. It doesn't make a pulpit wrong. And because somebody uses the printing press to preach false doctrine doesn't make the printing press wrong. It is the thing that is taught that is wrong. And because somebody preaches a false doctrine doesn't make the printing press wrong. And because somebody preaches a false doctrine over the radio doesn't make the radio wrong. It is the thing that he preaches that is wrong. The radio is still all right; and the same thing with the chart and the classes. So these are not wrong; it's the thing that emenates from them that is wrong. It is false doctrine. And so it's the false doctrine that's wrong, in reality, and not these things at all, for these are still *the means by which the teaching is done.* He hasn't touched it top, edge, side, nor bottom; and he will not touch it. That is the best he can do, and the very best any of his brethren can do. They just don't live that can do anything with it.

But he say 1 Peter 4:11 takes out the chart — the chart is not mentioned. 1 Peter 4:11 takes out the radio because the radio is not mentioned. And 1 Peter 4:11 takes out the printing press, the pulpit, because they're not mentioned. Don't you see? It takes them all out together. Too bad. If he had more time, he might have done better.

Now, I was really amused by his parallel. I showed how the matter of playing on the instrument has not parallel with singing, nor with class teaching, because *playing is not a means of singing.* Here we have the means of singing (pointing to blackboard) — song book, voice parts, the singing schools, invitation songs. Things of that kind are means by which we sing, but *playing* is *not a means of singing.* But playing has its own means, various instruments — the organ, the harp, banjo, or the violin. But he said, "I will give you a parallel on them", and here is his parallel: "Go, play on instruments, and sing". All right, now his parallel: "Go, divide into classes, and teach". Now, if that's parallel, I will give you a third one. "Go, get you radio microphone, and preach." Now, if one of those is parallel the other is. Cecil knew that wasn't parallel. He couldn't do any better — that is the very best he could do; and none of his brethren could do any better than that. *That's the only thing on earth he could do.* They can't get any further along than that, and they cannot draw any parallels; for that is it, and that is not a parallel. "Go, play on instruments and sing". You have two co-ordinate elements of music made. but when you say, "Go, divide into classes and teach", you do not have another co-ordinate element with teach. You only have a *means of teaching,* and *arrangement for teaching.* But *playing on an instrument is not an arrangement by which to sing.* It is a separate, co-ordinate element of music made that God didn't authorize. It is not a means of singing; it is not an arrangement for singing at all; but classes are simply an arrangement for teaching just like getting a microphone is an arrangement for preaching; and neither of them is parallel with playing on an instrument.

Cecil, can't you beat that? Well, maybe I shouldn't expect it. Really, I don't.

(Chart No. 2) And then he came to the judging of Israel. I was really amused at him here. He did just what I thought he would do. Now, here we have the tribes of Israel. I showed, according to the arrangement, that they had a number of teachers placed over Israel to judge them and to make known to them the law of God and his statutes; and to teach them the way they should do and the work that they should perform. And there were numbered 603,550 men from 21 years old and upward, who were able to go to war, besides all of the others which would probably number three times that many if all were put together. But just taking this number, we find a suggestion was made to put the judges, or the teachers, over the thousands, judges over the hundreds, judges over fifties, judges over the tens. When you take that number and put judges over the thousands, you have 603 judges; judges over the hundreds, you have 6,035; and judges over the fifties, you have 12,071; judges over the tens, you have 60,355. Therefore you have a total of 79,064 judges over these men in the congregation of Israel. I said that that judging, that teaching, could not be carried on unless some was done simultaneously, because if the people had to wait for those men to operate in consecutive order, they would have to wait just as long as they would have if they had to wait for Moses in the first place; and, consequently, it wouldn't take any burden off the people whatsoever. They would still have the same burden, waiting for the next man that they would have in the first place, waiting for Moses. And so in order for those to operate, there would be some simultaneous teaching. And I showed that the command to "teach" in the Old Testament did not specify an arrangement of this kind, but this arrangement was included in the command to teach. And if this sort of an arrangement upon a scale like that, as broad as that is, involving 79,064 teachers or judges, could be embraced in the word "teach" in the Old Testament, then why couldn't our dozen Sunday School classes be embraced in the word "teach" in the New Testament?

Oh, he says that was under the law; the church hadn't been established. I didn't say it was in the church. I gave it as a parallel, and I showed you that the word "teach" in the Old Testament involved that. And if the word "teach" in the Old Testament could include that why couldn't it include classes here? Tell us, Cecil, why it couldn't. You didn't even touch the argument. You talked all around it, and you didn't even say a word about the actual argument. You missed it completely.

But he says, "Now, the reason for that was the burden was too heavy." Well if the burden, then, was too heavy for us today, would it be all right for us to divide into classes? Huh? If we have the same reason, would it be all right? I makes no difference what the reason was, they had simultaneous teaching. I didn't give this as a parallel in every respect. In fact, I showed that things might be parallel in one part and not parallel in others; and he admitted that last night that things may be parallel in one point but not parallel in another. And so it's not parallel from the standpoint of the reason, but it is parallel from the standpoint of simultaneous teaching; and that's where he says the sin is. That's where the sin is.

Well, "they chose able men, and there weren't any sisters there." Yes, I know that they chose able men. Again, I said that they were not parallel in all parts. I didn't claim this to authorize women teachers. I used this to show the *parallel on simultaneous teaching.* You talked about everything else except the simultaneous teaching. Come back, Cecil, and talk about the thing upon which I based the argument. You admitted that things can be parallel in one point and not parallel in others. You can look at me if you want to. yes, sir, you admit that things can be parallel in one point and not be parallel in another. So I didn't say these were parallel in all points, but I did show it parallel in this point, the point of simultaneous teaching; and he hasn't touched it, and he will not touch it. Oh, but these were "all the tribes of Israel." Yes, but there was *but one congregation,* wasn't there? How many congregations of Israel were there?

You brought up Bros. A. E. Emmons over at Birmingham. I don't think that Bro. Emmons is there, but he was there some years ago. But he read a little bulletin from him about the small per cent in the attendance at Wednesday night meetings, and how disheartening the thing might be. And some brother handed me a note stating that the first time he attended service down here at Union City, where your moderator preaches, that *he didn't even have enough for Wednesday night service* — that they had to go home without it. So what does that prove?

Colossians 2:14, John 1:17 — the law of Moses was nailed to the cross. He said, "If he found the authority under Moses, why that still wouldn't mean anything." Well, I didn't go back to show the church existed under Moses. I was simply drawing parallels. But your brethren go back there. Did you ever hear the "rain argument" on Deuteronomy? "My doctrine shall drop as the rain." The rain all comes down on all the herbs and trees and everything just alike. Everyone gets his own part, and you don't have to grab your dishpan and go out and get some of it to bring in to water the little flowers with and the little green grass, but they all get what they need." Did you ever hear your brethren make that argument, Cecil? They went back to the Old Testament after that, and that's only one of the many they go back for. Why, certainly I didn't go back there to prove the church existed back there by the law of Moses. I went back there to draw a parallel on simultaneous teaching. There is no way around it. Absolutely no way around it: Then one more point — that's just about what time I have, and that gets everything he said. Acts 5:25 "The men who are standing in the temple and speaking to the people." I said that here's a plurality of men. They are standing and teaching; plurality of men standing (present tense), and teaching (present tense). If it had said they stood and taught the people, you wouldn't know when it was done. It might have been last week that one of them spoke, and it might have been last month that the other spoke, and it might have been last year for another, because the passage wouldn't have indicated anything about it. But it said these men "are standing and teaching," present tense; a plurality of speakers in the present tense — standing and teaching. And he said, "I'll give him a parallel that upsets that whole thing." And he went back to Acts 2:6 and 7 on which he was already blasted last night. "The multitude came together and was confounded because," he said, "they heard them speak in their own tongues", present tense. *Heard* them
—126—

speak, *present tense.* Cecil, are you going to go all they way on that present tense like you did at Taft? I just wondered. I'll wait till your next speech and see if you go all the way on the present tense like you did at Taft. If you don't, I am going to tell it on you. All right, but he said, "Whether that's present tense or not, this one is." Verse 7 — "Are not all these *which speak* Galileans". Yes, sir, there were different men there with different languages, and they said, "How hear we every man in our own tongue". Now how "heard" we, but how "hear" we, present tense. *We hear* every man in our own tongue, some in one language and some in another. Some are being taught in one language, and some in another. I take it that there was a plurality of speakers there addressing different groups of different languages and with different tongues. That gets it.

He came to Luke 24:19 but didn't have time to develop it. I don't have time to develop any more. (I have about a half minute, I believe that's right. Is that right?) Keep in mind now, we have four things — five things here: (Chart No. 1) Go, Baptize, Sing, Teach, and Play — all of these have means by which they are done. The means are included in the command that is authorized. The means of travel are included in the command to *go.* The means of baptizing are included in the command to *baptize.* The means of singing are included in the command to *sing.* The means of teaching are included in the command to *teach;* and the means of making mechanical instruments are included in the command to *play,* if we had that command. But there is no command, and so that isn't parallel, proven by the fact that it isn't in the book, but all these others are. But you cannot take the word "play", put it up here in "sing" and make it parallel with "song books" nor with "voice parts" nor with "singing schools", nor "invitation songs", because "play" is not a means by which singing is done. But the radio, the pulpit, the chart, printing press, and the classes are means by which teaching is done. If you teach in the pulpit, printing press, radio, chart, classes, you are still doing nothing but *teach,* and God said, "Teach." Classes are simply an arrangement by which the teaching is done, and, therefore, only a means. And you *teach,* and that's what the Lord said do — "Teach". And in the command to teach you have the authority for it. Thank you.

Abercrombie's Second Speech
Third Night — December 6, 1951 (Negative)

Ladies and Gentlemen, Fellow Moderators, Bro. Porter:

I'm happy to be before you once more denying the proposition which has been read in your hearing tonight. Bro. Porter is here affirming that it is scriptural for the church to come together to organize a Sunday School, to divide up into classes with a staff of teachers, plurality of teachers, and men and women teaching at the same time those respective classes of the church. Now, that is what he is searching for.

He quibbled about men mentioning some things that he says are extraneous matter. I said last evening and times before, we tried to keep him to the proposition and he would not. He begged for other matters to be brought in and he begged the question with such as this.

Here I want to introduce again a few things from Bro. Phillips splendid tract. It's a review of the debate he had with a man on musical instruments, and here is the same argument that Bro. Phillips made when those things were hurled at him. (Bro. Porter makes the same arguments.) "Use made of a chart or blackboard in teaching; a notebook, a tuning fork, a time stake in singing; a meeting house, pews and carpets on the floors for the convenience and the comforts for the Christians when they assemble for worship are not now on trial. Even though it might be proven wrong to use any one or all of these, that does not prove it either right or wrong to use instruments of music in divine worship when Christians assemble", etc. He says that those who bring such in are just simply begging the question, and that's all it is, just begging the question. "Misery loves company", he said, "any time I *am* charges with sinning in any of those things I will defend the use I make of such", and so you can see why such as been brought in. If he'd stick right to the precious word of God and show from the word of God his practice, then such things would not be necessary. But he knows that he cannot make his cause even look pretty good, without going to something else and covering up the issue. That's all it's for; it is a camouflage.

And now then we turn to Exodus 18, and we wish to notice something else. Incidentally, in this arrangement he has found he said, "This is it. This is the parallel between what I do today in the churches of Christ, here is simultaneous teaching." I haven't heard him offer yet one scripture for women teaching. I waited. I wanted to hear him make and give us a scripture for women teaching. Friends, this man is afraid to introduce anything along that line. He is, he should have introduced it tonight. Why, he knows that he cannot prove his practice. Women teaching belongs in that Sunday School that he has, and he was afraid to introduce a passage of scripture about women teaching, we're going to give you a prophetess. All right, let's look at it. Why didn't you notice this? Your proposition required it, and if you are going to stick to your parallel in Exodus you would have used it. Here is the reason he didn't use it. Exodus 15:20, "And Miriam, the prophetess", (Exodus, just the 15th chapter. He was reading from the 18th.), "Miriam, the prophetess, the sister of Aaron, took a timbrel in hand; and all the women went out after her with timbrels and with dance." Going to dance now in Sunday School, and going to have women blowing all kinds of things. Why didn't you make the parallel complete? There it is, in Exodus, and he overlooked that. He didn't want to read it. No, but there you find musical instruments in the parallel.

And concerning the Taft incident in 1 Chron. 25, I did not offer that as proof for any practice that I do. I so stated in that debate, and he continually misrepresents. I had it in black and white when I said it, (I knew he would twist it that way). I had it in black and white, and said, "I do not use this for proof of anything that I practice, but because Bro. Porter said it's not in the Bible I'm showing him that it is." That is the reason that I used it. He said, "he used it for his singing school, and there were musical instruments in it." No sir, that wasn't the case anyway whatsoever. That wasn't the case.

But now then we have Miriam, the prophetess. A prophetess is a teacher, and she is in the Sunday School with all the women. Notice — just women, but have an orchestra and the women are dancing. Now that is the parallel. That is the things that he gets into because he can't find anything better. He will never find anything better than that.

Porter says, "1 Cor. 14:31, he says nothing in that about remaining in one group." Friends, I want you to read that passage of scripture tonight and see if you can in the fondest imagination that you might have, conceive of how those people could be taught if they didn't remain in one group. And Paul positively commanded the teachers to speak one by *one* by *one* to all. Now notice — *"one by one that all may learn"* — "Speak one by one that all may learn and all may be comforted." God commanded that the church in those teaching services, all of them that assemble hear *all* of the *teachers*. He says that you don't have to do that. He says that you don't have to remain in one group for that to be done. *I challange him to show that it can be done otherwise when you follow what Paul says.* He is not following what Paul says. He sets them up all talking at once, and divided them into classes. The apostle, by the inspiration of God, said, "Speak one by one that *all may learn* and *all may be comforted,"* just like we are speaking here tonight. He speaks, and I speak, and so forth, but all hear; and that is what Paul authorized. One audience and one speaker speaking at a time, and that's what Paul is teaching there. He knows that it is a death blow to his class system, and verse 35, did he notice that? Oh, but he is going to notice everything that I said, but you see how he shies off women teachers. He applies 1 Cor. 14:31 to his classes He said, "Yes, that applies to our classes." I told him that *verse 35* goes along with it. *It knocks his women out of the Sunday School classes — he won't have it.* He is afraid of that issue. I know what I am talking about. You see how he shied off of it.

Now then, "Shelbourne is doing scriptural work". Why did you present it? Why did you bring it up? "Shelbourne is doing a scriptural work". I believe as far as the work and teaching is concerned and in arrangement, and the way it is taught is scriptural. It is what I do, teach one by one in undivided assemblies.

Then, "he brought up Kellog and his teaching." Yes, with that — what he said — Kellog ruins Bro. Porter's position. Bro. Porter wouldn't allow men to go into a class that is taught by women and hear her teach, and there is on record. Bro. Gardner Hall in the "Way of Life" paper — said that this ought to be supervised and that all teaching ought to be supervised. *I wonder how they are going to supervise teaching of the women.* Men can't even listen in; and another thing, my friends, the consistency! He's so consistent, you know! and women are immune from oversight by the elders according to his teachings, because it is a sin for a man to go into a woman's classes. Just put the lock on, she just has to clam up when he goes in. "Could preach over a radio if men wouldn't listen in!" How are the elders going to oversee such as that? Yes, he has established a female ministry for women only, an order unknown to the word of God.

Yes, brethren, concerning those who are leaving, of course that is not germane to the issue; but, he knows that many are leaving him. An occasional one, two, three, or four, or something like that leave us. Yes sir, but they are leaving him. We are leading them out of this digression in Birmingham all along. And he talked about "this assembly" again. I am speaking to one assembly. I am speaking to a multitude just like Jesus did, no division into classes for a plurality of simultaneous teaching. Jesus didn't do that. He didn't offer an example where Jesus did any part of simultaneous teaching. No sir, but we will deal with that in just a moment.

Porter said he didn't know who was in the basement. The other night he made a lot of play over here about "Where did you ever hear me say a woman couldn't teach men?" He didn't know who was in the basement, but if just women were in the basement a woman could teach them, couldn't she? That's his doctrine. Could she teach those women in the basement from where I stand here? Oh, no! Couldn't do that. Be a sin to do that — she would teach men then.

All right, "Sunday School class" — Said, "if the Sunday School class assemble, if they convene, but they did not go into an assembly." The practice is just as false. *The practice is just as sinful. If that changes it any, why then couldn't the women teach the men's Bible class if that changes it any? I want to hear more about that.* We want to hear something in this discussion about women teachers. He didn't mention it in his two talks, not once that I remember. If he did I didn't catch it.

Radio and classes are not parallel as I showed. Classes are violating the principles taught in the word of God, and he knows that his women teaching in Sunday School violates the word of God. He has shied off of this entirely. He knows that it goes along with 1 Cor. 14:31 — "It is a shame for women to speak in the church". Yes, he's caught. He is a drowning man. Porter sets aside the Lord's plan for a human plan.

Porter said that he was following me last night. If he was he sure did get lost, way behind. Somebody needs to send out a searching party for him.

Porter's doctrine on "must" is certainly a digressive argument. With the things that he propounded to me in the beginning of this discussion he couldn't meet a Christian church preacher under the sun because on the same promise he couldn't find a scripture in the word of God that says you "must not use musical instruments to accompany singing." "Must not play on instruments", he couldn't find it to save his soul. He finds where it says sing. He says that excludes playing. I find where it says teach. I find in every example of teaching, they never divided into classes. I find where Paul said, in such assemblies of the church, says speak one by one to all that all may learn and that all may be comforted. I find in the word of God for women not to teach in such assemblies of the church. He violates all these principles, ignores all these examples, and then comes back and asks for such as that which would even prove musical instruments scriptural. There is where he belongs. Even his parallel in the Old Testament puts what woman, gets the woman in there according to his parallel, and have musical instruments with her. He wouldn't take the parallel far enough. "It's over there, there it is", he says, and so that shows where the apostle teaches that they should remain together. If they didn't remain together they wouldn't hear all the teachers speaking one by one, "Speak one by one that all may learn and all may be comforted." They wouldn't hear all the teachers as Paul commanded if they didn't remain together. He says, "Find where it says to remain together." There is where it says it. And so in the context they wouldn't be able to hear all the teachers. The teachers were commanded to speak one by one to all. If they didn't remain together they couldn't hear all the teachers. God wanted all the church to be edified by all the teaching that was done in that assembly. Women weren't allowed to do any of it. He says in his proposition, he says, "Women can do some of the teaching in the class system." His practice will not stand up.

Then concerning the singing school: In the last discussion I met Bro. Gus Nichols, Bro. Gus Nichols trying to improve his debating ability on this subject has been listening to that debate, (The Taft, Tenn. Debate). and when we pressed him on that he made almost the same statement. He said, "You can't find it in the Bible," and I proved by the word of God, by the same scripture, that they had song instruction in the Bible. He said it wasn't there. I showed him that it was in there, in the Bible if you please not to justify anything that I do, but he said it wasn't there. He said, "Porter made a mistake on that. You won't get me into that." He made almost the same blunder. He just said he found a Sunday School where I found a Singing School in the Old Testament — in the Bible, and so Gus just left that out. He thought he was wise. But he got into a trap just the same.

He said, about a brother he talked to, "he had no knowledge." I expect you could talk to a lot of brethren around here that don't have any knowledge about Montevallo, Ala. The brother he talked to; he said had no knowledge about that case down there — that all — women church and the woman conducting the service there. You could talk to a lot of the brethren here that don't have any knowlege about it. They have heard of it now, but they don't really have any knowledge about it. *I do. I went over there.* Is it scriptural? If it is scriptural in Montevallo, Ala. would it be at Monnett? If it is scriptural at Montevallo would it be at Montgomery? They wouldn't have it in Montgomery, They would throw it out in Birmingham, Ala. Bro Porter would condemn it in Monnett. "Sisters just disban that thing over there. That is a shame to the church. Come on over here where I am." That is what Bro. Porter would teach.

If three women fell out of an airplane, could they worship God?" Could they preach the gospel and baptize, and set the church in order, and after they set the church in order could they ordain elders? And then after they ordain elders *baptize men?* Could they continue to teach those sinners whom they had baptized? How about that? That puts him in a pickle, doesn't it?

All right, to, 1 Cor. 14:31 —

(Moderator: 12 minutes)

This keeps the church together. The classes violate the precious word of God. 1 Peter 4:11, this takes the classes out, because it violates the scriptures. "If any man speaks let him speak as the oracles of God." That's the way I used it. It takes them out because it violates the word of God. He twisted that some. He said that the dividing was not parallel to playing, or something to that effect. There is clearly a parallel — two additions: *Divide* into the classes and teach; *Play* on instruments and sing. There is a parallel. *There are two additions.* One is *dividing into classes* and then teaching. The other is, *adding an instrument,* playing on an instrument and singing. Two additions — they are parallel — but if that doesn't suit him they are

—133—

included in Matt. 15:8-9, "But in vain do they worship me teaching for doctrines the commandments of men". Both of them are commandments of men. And on this same premise we would bring in the Missionary Society as a means of teaching, the same way that he brings in and justifies classes. He says it's a means to the end to teach. Just the same way the Christian Church argues that the Missionary Society is a means of preaching the gospel. Everybody can see that parallel. Both of them are human institutions to do what the Lord told the church to do. God does not allow such as that. His logic justifies Missionary Societies. "Old Testament judges" — yes, women teachers. He left that out, but he takes the judges or rulers. Better look out now, you are going to have *women judges or rulers in the church – women rulers, women elders.* Now he has got them ruling. He doesn't believe that women can rule. Deborah, an Old Testament *prophetess judges Israel and was a ruler in Israel.* Sometimes they bring that up, but he won't do it. Afraid of it! He knows that his practice won't stand it and his teaching won't. "Miriam", yes, "if Moses could do that, why can't we." "If Moses could do that why can't we", he says. *Well, if Miriam could teach those women and play on instruments and dance, why can't we?* It's ridiculous what a man of his intelligence gets into. My friends, his weakness in this discussion is not on account of his inability and his lack of talent. It is because he doesn't have the truth. "Selected able men". He couldn't find a woman there. Well, we have supplied it.

Now then, we turn to Acts 5:25. They are standing teaching the people. All right, what did he do with Acts 2:7? Not one thing, but got himself into one of the biggest messes you have ever seen. *Why, there he has set up twelve men speaking at the same time to one assembly.* You remember the sixth verse says, "The multitude came together", and it says, "Are not all these which speak Galileans?" Parallel with the language of Acts 5:25 — twelve men, if you please. The multitude came together and the only way, according to Porter, that that could have been done, they had to divide into classes according to the language. When a group authorizes one to speak for them it IS Scriptural and gramatical to say "they spoke". In Acts 4 we find there another parallel to this concerning what the word of God teaches, and so we will at this point turn to the Acts of Apostles, the 4th chapter, and read just a few verses here showing the plural, how the plural is used. "And as *they spake* unto the people the priest and the captain of the temple and the Saducees came upon them, being grieved that they taught the people and preached through Jesus the resurrection from the dead." I admit that "they spake" is in the past tense. but notice, friends "and as they spake unto the people" — notice the plural; there was Peter and John teaching, "As they spake unto the people the priest and the captain of the temple and Saducces came upon them. But the 3rd chapter shows that Peter was the only one doing the preaching. John concurred with what Peter said, and the scriptures said "they spake." And back over here in the 3rd chapter it says that they all "came together in Solomon's porch." They were all together. *So now according to Porter's interpretation of Acts 5:25 we have two men teaching the same assembly at one time.* And that may be confusing and he doesn't allow that — he doesn't believe in two preachers or twelve preachers speaking in the same audience at one time, and that's what he has gotten out of the whole thing, and it has ruined his position entirely.

Now then, to Mark 7:14-18 — introduced to prove classes. "Jesue taught classes", he said, verse 14. Jesus taught the multitude. Verse 16 shows when he quit teaching the multitude and in verse 17 we see Jesus going into a house. He says that is simultaneous teaching. Can anybody with a grain of gumption see that? "That's simultaneous teaching, he says. Jesus taught a multitude and then he dismissed them or quit teaching them. Didn't set anybody up over them to teach them at all. Then he went into a house and the disciples came over there and then Jesus taught them something else, and that's simultaneous teaching! That's his class system, he says. That's proof, isn't it! Good night a living! Notice all the teachers: Jesus and the disciples were over in the house. They left the multitude, and did Jesus put the Scribes and the Pharisees over there teaching that multitude? There Jesus and all the teachers were over in the house — he said that's simultaneous teaching! Now that's the case in every one of the things he brought up. The teachers were in the house with Jesus. He had left the multitude and nobody was teaching them. He's got to find something better than that.

Now then teaching apart from others, use Acts 18:26. There was Aquila and Priscilla, took Apollos unto them and taught him the way of the Lord more perfectly. Now there, if he wants a parallel to Sunday School, there he has it. Yes it is. Will you have it? They have a woman teacher there, and they did just like Jesus did; They withdrew from a multitude. Apollos was over there preaching in the synagogue, and when Apollos finished, Aqula and Priscilla took him unto then and taught him the way of the Lord more perfectly. But Bro. Porter won't have that, but if He's going to find anything in the Bible that resembles his Sunday School with women teaching in it, that's it, but he won't have it. It's the only thing in the Bible that would resemble it, to get women teachers in, but he finds a woman teaching a man and *he's made a law where God made none and said, "Women can't teach men in classes."* And he says that's private. That's private! Women can teach men in private. Our Sunday School is private but you can't teach in my Sunday School where there are men! That's consistency, isn't it?

(Moderator: Five minutes.)

The transfiguration — of all the ridiculous suppositions he uses as proof of the public meetings of the church in class teaching, this is the limit! After six days he has taken Peter, James and John, his brother apart and bringeth them up into a high mountain. Jesus was transfigured before them, and Moses and Elijah were seen talking to Jesus. Luke 9:28 tells us that they went up into the mountain to pray, and verse 32 tells us that the disciples went to sleep, (Sunday School class!) but awoke in time to see the glorious sight. Had a miracle up there. And in the Taft debate Bro. Porter, about the first position he took on 1 Cor. 14 was C. R. Nichols' position that there is not an illustration or assembly on earth like that today. Why, that had miraculous gift in it, etc. And them he reached over there and took up Acts 2 and tried to prove Sunday School from that, and we showed that it had miraculous gifts in that, and according to his own position he knocked it out. And, so, if he still sticks with that he knocks this out too, for they had a miracle on top of the mountain — came down the next day, and the disciples were trying to perform a miracle and couldn't for the lack of faith, and then Jesus had to get the job done, and he says that's our class system. Oh, my! What men will grab at when they are drowning.

All right, in verse 33 Peter suggested (here is something else this Sunday School class suggested), Peter suggested that they build three tabernacles or churches. Let's build three "not knowing what he said," — just like a Sunday School class, not knowing what they are doing! In verse 37 we learn that the next day they walked down the mountain. Now he's abandoning that class upon the top of the mountain. There is the class coming down the mountain, and accidently they run into a class (?) he calls it, a mixed promiscus multitude at the bottom, and the disciples didn't know what it was all about, and he calls that a teaching service. It looks more like a Holiness healing service that backfired. They couldn't cast out a lunatic, and that's what they were arguing about, and the disciples didn't know why they couldn't do it, and Jesus said, "Because of you lack of faith'. And there are the classes down there (?). And another thing about that, there was plurality of the disciples, a plurality of teachers, over one class, the multitude, and he said that's a class down at the bottom. And we find a plurality of teachers and *they* (plural) *they* were arguing and so there, even in their class he's got a *plurality of teachers over one class*. He won't have that Some parallel, isn't it? And as they are walking down the mountain talking with Jesus and Jesus is charging them to tell no man what they had seen. The disciples ask him about Elias, Mark 9:1-11. When they reached the foot of the mountain, or wherever the disciples were, he saw a great multitude about them. When the people saw Jesus they were amazed and came running to Jesus, verse 15. The Scribes were asking questions of the disciples. Jesus asked, "Why question ye with them?" — verse 16. He was quickly informed that the disciples had failed to cure a child with a bumb fit or was a lunatic, Matt. 17:15 — Jesus cured the child and when Jesus was apart or away from the multitude in a house (see Matt. 17:19 and Mark 9:28) the disciples asked him, why they couldn't cast out the dumb spitit. In Mark 9:19 he said, "Oh faithless generation". In Matt. 17:20 Jesus said unto them, "Because of your unbelief you couldn't cast it out." This part of the occurence is the only thing that looks like Sunday School. That has teachers without faith in God's word, faith in God's word will do away with the Sunday School. 1 Cor. 14:35 — will get the women out and the 31st verse stops the classes and teaches altogether as God has commanded. I thank you kindly for listening.

Porter's Second Affirmative Speech
Fourth Night — December 7, 1951

Brethren Moderators, Bro. Abercrombie, Ladies and Gentlemen:

I am very sorry that last night I seemed to disturb Bro. Cecil so much by not leading out on a discussion of the question of women teachers. It seemed to appear that, perhaps, he had his reply written out mostly to counteract a speech of that kind, and since the speech wasn't made, then his reply didn't fit, but it so happens that I have two parts in my proposition just as he had two parts in his: One, the idea of arranging into groups; and then the other, the women teachers. I took them in the order in which they were place in the proposition. So last night I gave my attention to the matter of arranging into groups as being authorized by the scriptures, and all of that blowing that Cecil did in his final speech that Porter is afraid of the woman question, that Porter shies away from the woman question, and various things along that line, was wasted and misspent effort, because I am sure that you will be able to judge for yourself for yourself how badly scared Porter really is.

The question which we are discussing, according to the proposition just read is that "that practice of arranging into groups the people that come together to be taught by the church and using both men and women in that teaching," or to teach these groups, "is authorized by the scriptures." That means, of course, two women may teach some of the groups. The proposition doesn't say that she can teach all of them. So tonight I want to introduce some affirmative arguments along that line, and when I shall have done so, then I shall take up the speech that was made at the closing of the session last night. I shall not try during this session to introduce everything that might be said respecting women teachers. There isn't time for a consideration of all of those scriptures that might be use. But we shall take a few and endeavor to get them before you plainly and simply that you may understand them and thus get the truth of God into your hearts and minds along this line.

So I shall pay my attention to the question of women teachers that Cecil thought I was so afraid of. And, in the first place, I call your attention to the fact that women are commanded to teach. Well, I am sure that I give you this quotation, but I want to turn and read it to you from the book of Almighty God, found in the book of Titus, the second chapter, and begin reading with about the first verse. "But speak thou the things which become sound doctrine; that the aged men be sober, grave, temperate, sound in faith, in charity, in patience. The aged women likewise, that they be in behavior as becometh holiness, and not false accusers, not given to much wine, teachers of good things; that they may teach the young women to be sober, to love their husbands, to love their children, to be discreet, chaste, keepers at home, good, obedient to their husbands, that the word of God be not blasphemed". Now, you note in this passage that the apostle Paul, writing to Titus, instructs him to tell others the things that are here enumerated. Reference is made to four different groups in this passage — the aged men, the aged women, the young women, and the young men. And Paul in the passage commands women to teach here own sex, for he says, "The aged women likewise, that they be in behavior as becometh holiness, not false accusers, not given to much wine, teachers of good things, that they may teach the young women to be sober, to love their husbands, to love their children, to be discreet, chaste, keepers at home, good, obedient to their own husbands that the word of God be not blasphemed." Thus God commands in this passage the aged women to teach the young women, and we have, therefore, a specific commandment for women teaching. The apostle Paul commands that this be done, and, of course, the teaching may be done in various ways. The woman might go around from house to house and teach one person at a time. If she followed that sort of course, spending one hour with each woman, she could teach 30 women in 30 hours, but if she had those 30 women together, *she could teach the same 30 women the same things in one hour.* And thus we find that more teaching could be accomplished. The job could be done more readily by her teaching more than one person at a time. So if she taught 30 persons in one hour, she would accomplish the same amount of teaching that she would do to 30 persons in 30 hours if she took them one by one.

And besides, Cecil has admitted already that an arrangement of that kind would not be any violation of any argument that he has based upon 1 Cor. 14. As you remember the other night when I asked for him to tell us something about what a

"Church assembly" meant, he referred to Matt. 18:20. "Where two or three are gathered in my name," the Lord said, "I am there with them". He said that is a church assembly. So I asked him, "Suppose those two or three were women?" He came back and said that it wouldn't be a church assembly if the women were grouped. If the women came together like that, it would not be a church assembly. Yet all the arguments he makes against women teaching concerns women teaching in church assemblies. Since, therefore, if a number of women came together, they do not constitute a church assembly, according to Cecil, then a woman could teach her own sex in a group like that without violating any passage he has given. Certainly that is the predicament Cecil has himself into now. He is either going to have to say that a group of that kind is a church assembly or he is going to have to admit that women can teach in it, one or the other! Now, you come, Cecil, tonight and tell us whether or not you will take one or the other. You have said that women gathered together do not constitute a church assembly, and that you didn't include women when you made that statement. All right then, if they do not constitute a church assembly, why could not a woman teach in that group? Why could she not teach other women in a group of that kind since, according to you, they do not constitute a church assembly?

Then I will pass from that to a second argument based on a statement made by Paul in 1 Tim. 2:12 in which he says, "I suffer not a woman to teach, nor to usurp authority over the man, but to be in silence." Cecil has used this passage a number of times. So I come now to a consideration of the passage here — "I suffer not a woman to teach, nor to usurp authority over the man," Now, note that in this passage there are two things forbidden. First, she is forbidden to teach. In the second place, she is forbidden to usurp authority. However, if we stop there, we find ourselves in direct conflict with other statements made in God's book. If I just read the passage that Paul uttered. "I suffer not a woman to teach", and stop there without any modification, without any modifying phrase, or anything of that kind, then I have a direct conflict between that passage and the one just given in Titus 2, for in the 2nd chapter of Titus Paul commanded women to teach. But here he says, "I suffer not a woman to teach." Is that a conflict between two passages? No, no, there is no conflict. The woman is certainly allowed to teach her children. Cecil wouldn't deny that. And if she is allowed to teach her children, you can't take that without some modifications. You can't take it unqualifiedly. So there must be something to modify it. There must be something to qualify it. You can't just read, "I suffer not a woman to teach", and stop there. If you do, you throw it into direct conflict with a commandment that Paul has given in Titus 2. So a woman certainly can teach her children. She can exercise dominion over her children, and this passage certainly does not forbid a thing of that kind. Yet Paul says, "I suffer not a woman to teach nor to usurp authority". But we find that both those infinitives are modified by a prepositional phrase. That propositional phrase is "over the man". I'm insisting that that propositional phrase modifies both infinitives, and to get a parallel with that statement, I turn to Acts 4:18, in which we are told that they commanded the apostles, the disciples upon that occasion not to do something. "They commanded them not to speak at all nor teach in the name of Jesus". Now, if we just read that without any qualifying terms, without any phrase, "they commanded them not to speak at all", they couldn't even say "hello" to one another on the streets. They would not have been allowed to utter any kind of vocal sound whatsoever. "They commanded them not to speak at all nor teach in the name of Jesus."

And so I have upon the blackboard a diagram of these two sentences tonight. (Chart No. 3) Here we have Acts 4:18, "They commanded them not to speak at all nor teach in the name of Jesus". And we have in this sentence, first, the subject, "They". "Commanded" is the verb or the predicate, and "them" is the direct object, or in some grammers called object complement. We have a compound infinitive phrase, "to speak nor to teach." "To speak not at all." And "not to speak at all nor to teach." And here we have those connected by the conjunction, "nor". "To speak not at all nor to teach". And they are both modified by the prepositional phrase, "in the name of Jesus". These compose what some grammarians call "the objective complement." All right then, "They commanded them not to speak at all nor to teach in the name of Jesus." Shall we make "in the name of Jesus" modify "teach" only, or should we let it modify both infinitives? "They commanded them not to speak at all nor to teach in the name of Jesus." According to Cecil's theology along this line, you would have to make it modify teach and leave the other out completely. Therefore, they cannot utter any kind of vocal sound; they could not even speak to each other on the street, for they commanded them not to speak *at all*. But the fact is "they commanded them not to speak at all in the name of Jesus", nor to teach in the name of Jesus." The expression, "in the name of Jesus," the prepositional phrase, modifies both infinitives in that case and simply suggests to us that idea.

Well, in the other we have parallel. Paul said, "I suffer not woman to teach, nor to usurp authority over the man." "I" is the subject; "suffer" is the predicate or the verb; and "woman" is the object complement, and modified by the article "a", of course. And we have the compound infinitives, "to teach — to usurp authority." "Authority" is the object of the very "usurp" in that case. (Pointing to "usurp") This would be the other infinitive, and they are connected by the same conjunction "nor". "I suffer not a woman to teach nor to usurp authority over the man." Cecil makes this modify "usurp authority" and will not allow it to modify "teach." "I suffer not a woman to teach," *period*, so far as he is concerned. "Nor to usurp authority over the man." Therefore he makes it in direct conflict with Paul's commandment for a woman to teach. But the fact is "over the man" is a prepositional phrase which modifies the compound infinitive phrase, just as up in this case "in the name of Jesus Christ" modifies the compound infinitives, which are used as the objective complement. It suggests to us the fact that Paul taught: "I suffer not a woman to teach over the man nor to usurp authority over the man," both the infinitives being modified by the phrase, "over the man." Therefore the woman is allowed to teach in any capacity in which she does not teach over the man, in which she does not teach in any way to exercise authority over the man, or as some translations give it, "have dominion" or authority" over the man. I shall insist that he pay attention to that diagram. (Chart No. 4)

Now, we come to another part, and over here I have written upon the board, "Speaking forbidden in the church". 1 Cor. 14:34-35. This is the passage around which Cecil has traveled all the time, in which Paul said, "Let your women keep silence in the churches: for it is not permitted unto them to speak; but they are commanded to be under obedience, as also saith the law. And if they will learn anything, let them ask their husbands at home: for it is a shame for women to speak in the church." Now, you know that Cecil has been harping on that all the time, and he has been thinking Porter was afraid of it, and all of that. Well, we are going to see how scared Porter really is. Notice now, he says that "It is a shame for women to speak in the church." Now, that speaking which is forbidden upon that occasion is either *limited or unlimited.* If that speaking is *unlimited,* then she is not allowed to speak in any form or fashion in any assembly of the church, and that certainly would necessitate and involve a great many difficulties. If that's used *in an unlimited sense,* if a woman should respond to the invitation, come forward at the close of a gospel sermon, you could not have her to confess Jesus Christ in the assembly; for if that is unlimited, she would be violating that. She would *be doing that which is shameful if she made the confession* of Jesus Christ. So the only thing that could be done in a case of that kind would be to take her out on the front steps and have her make the confession out there. But when you do that you divide the assembly, and still send her to hell. So you can see that it cannot be an *unlimited* proposition at all. In fact, Cecil, under pressure, has finally said that *it is not unlimited,* that *he does not mean that it is unlimited.* Therefore, Cecil means that *under some circumstances* a woman *can speak in the assembly* of the church, and yet it not be shameful. He has said that she can do it. *It's not unlimited.* But he said it's limited to the speaking talked about in the context.

All right, so say I. We are perfectly agreed upon that. We agree that it's not an unlimited matter. We agree that it's limited to that which is discussed in the context. The thing, therefore, for us to find out is what is being discussed in the context — what type of speaking, what type of teaching, is revealed in the context that a woman cannot do. *Not every* kind, for Cecil has admitted that there is some kind she can do, even in *the assembly* of the church. That is not unlimited. So what kind is it, what type is it, that she cannot do, that is revealed in the context? Well, verse 34 says, "Let you women keep silence in the churches: for it is not permitted unto them to speak; but they are commanded to be *under obedience,* as also saith the law." Notice, how, the speaking prohibited is involved in the idea tht "they are commanded to be *under obedience,*" or as the Revised Version says, "in subjection." They are required to be *in subjection;* and any kind of speaking that takes her out of subjection to man, any kind of speaking that brings her out of that state of subjection to where she is *not subordinate to man,* and thus would be *teaching over the man,* excerising authority over the man, according to 1 Tim. 2:12, which I gave a while ago on the other passage, is the kind *of speaking that is forbidden in that passage.* She is not allowed to speak in such a way as not to be subjected to man, and that is the very kind of speaking she would be doing in the assembly as described there, if she addressed that assembly as a speaker would address an assembly — as I am addressing you now. If she took the stand and addressed that assembly that's made partly of men, because it's the whole church assembled in one place, and consequently, in the presence of men. She cannot become a *public preacher of the gospel.* If she became a public preacher, she would be *exercising authority over the man* and *would not be in subjection to man,* and that is the kind of speaking that is forbidden in 1 Cor. 14:34-35.

And to show you furthermore, that she can speak, Cecil has admitted she can sing. Yes, in the fourth place, *the woman can sing,* and Paul said in Col. 3:16 and Eph. 5:19 *when she sings she both speaks and teaches.* Therefore, when she sings *she speaks,* but *she can sing in the assembly,* and it is not a shame for her to do it. Therefore, she can do *some kinds of speaking in the assembly* which isn't a shame. And Cecil will admit that *she can confess Christ in the assembly.* It's not a shame to do that. So there's some speaking she can do in the assembly that's not a shame for her. And upon the same basis, I insist that she can teach her children, and in doing so, she is not taking herself out from subjection to man; she is not exercising authority over the man when she does. She can teach women, her own sex, without taking herself out of subjection to men. Therefore singing, confessing Christ, and teaching her own children and teaching women are not a violation of the prohibition laid down in 1 Cor. 14:34-35.

Now, I pass on to a consideration of the things uttered by my opponent last night. One thing I want you to keep in mind on 1 Cor. 14:31. Cecil has misquoted it so long that it is almost impossible for him not to. "You may all prophesy one by one *to all,* that all may learn and all may be comforted." And invariably he will get right back on that, regardless of how many times he reads it correctly. When he starts commenting on it, he will get that right back in to it. "You may all prophesy one by one *unto all,* that all may learn, and that all may be comforted." The words, "unto all", are the words supplied by Cecil. *He reads those words into it, and upon those words he makes his law* which God has not made; for the passage says not that they must remain in one assembly. Now, you watch him and see if he doesn't do that thing tonight.

On Acts 5:25, where we find about their standing and teaching in the temple, and I showed that there is a plurality of speakers. *"They are standing, they are teaching"* — present tense. Didn't say *they stood,* and *they taught,* but *they are standing, they are teaching.* Cecil came back with Acts 4:1 — "They spake unto the people." "As they spake unto the people". He said, "I admit that that's past tense." Cecil, here in this debate, has tried to array me against some of my brethren on some minor details or matters. As for example, "God's Woman", written by Bro. C. R. Nichol. And he had a great deal to say about that — if I didn't accept everything that Brother Nichol said in the book. Why of course, he had me arrayed against him, and he tried to made a great play upon that. Well, I'm sure that Brother Nichol would not claim infallibility, and Porter does not claim infallibility; and if I should write a book as large as "God's Woman," very likely I'd say something that Brother Nichol would not endorse whole-heartedly. I do not know of any person anywhere that would agree with me in all minor details, in detail of every subject, but what does that prove? Is there anything serious about that? Does that mean that I must repudiate Brother Nichol? Why, no, Brother Nichol is a great gospel preacher, one of the greatest gospel preachers and debaters of this time, or for many years gone by, and certainly he is a very close friend of mine. But trying to array me against him doesn't mean anything on earth, for we find that Cecil has arrayed Cecil against himself. In this passage, he says of Acts 4:1, "I admit that it is past tense." Cecil is learning. In the debate up at Taft, Tenn., Cecil brought up this passage, and others right along with it, and quoted, "They spake unto the people", and said, "present tense" — "present tense." And he came back speech after speech and session after session and continued to argue for it, although I showed him conclusively in various ways that it *was not present tense,* that it was past tense. He even introduced Goodspeed, I believe it was, who said, "as they *were speaking,"* and Cecil said "That shows that it is present tense." On and on — and he wanted that debate to occur in print just as it was spoken. I asked him if he wanted the "present tense" proposition to go in. All of that happened up there. But now he comes down here and says, "I admit that 'they spake' is past tense." Well, than you Cecil. I'm glad you are learning. If you keep on, you may learn some more things concerning this matter. And so we pass from that.

In the second chapter of Acts, the seventh verse, he said, "Porter has twelve men speaking at the same time to one assembly." Well, that wasn't true, but just granting his argument, if that assembly was arranged as this assembly is arranged tonight, then one man could not have addressed that assembly upon that occasion without the use of a public address system, which they did not have in that day. Cecil has been addressing various groups — some in one room, some in another, during this debate — although his proposition said that the people *must remain in one group*. "They must remain in one group". And yet he's going to hell upon his own proposition, because he has been speaking to different groups at the same time. So that could not have been done as he's doing it now on the day of Pentecost if they had been arranged as they are arranged here, for they had no public address system then.

Then I came to the judging of Israel, Exodus 18. (Chart number 2) I showed last night that in the judgment of Israel Moses' father-in-law suggested to Moses, in order to get away from the great burden placed upon him, he was wearing himself out and wearing the people out — that they place judges over the people to help them. There were numbered 603,550 men, 21 years old and upward. He said to place over those men a judge over the thousands, a judge over the hundreds, and a judge over the fifties and a judge over tens. And when we have a judge over thousands, we have 603 judges; judges over the hundreds, 6,035; judges over the fifties, 12,071; judges over the tens, 60,355; or a total of 79,064 judges, which Moses showed were teaching the law of God, making known to the people what they should do, the things that God demanded of them, and the work that they should perform and things of that kind. And I insisted that with that sort of arrangement there must be *simultaneous teaching*. You can't have that many men operating under a condition of that kind without having simultaneous teaching, for if one man followed the other consecutively, the people would wear out just as much waiting for the next man as they would if they waited for Moses in the first place.

Cecil came back and said, "Well, that doesn't fit your Sunday School class because there were no women there. It said, 'able men'; there were no women there." Well, I showed at the very beginning, I didn't claim it parallel in every point. Cecil has admitted that things man be parallel in one point but not parallel in other points, and I gave that as a *parallel of simultaneous teaching* — not on other points, but *on that point*. And it does parallel that point. But Cecil said, "There were no women there." Then, in his next speech, he came back and said, "Why, we will just complete the parallel" — and he put Miriam into it. He went back to Exodus 15, that Miriam went forth with timbrels and dances, and said I would have to take that. Why, I thought, Cecil, you said there were no women in it. Then you turned right around shoved Miriam into it, when you said, in the first place, there were no women there. The fact is *Miriam had no connection with that arrangement whatever*. It is an entirely distinct thing, and Cecil hasn't touched it, and he'll not be able to touch it. He's as helpless as helpless can be when it comes to that.

He also wanted to know, if I appealed to Moses, why not play and dance, as in the case of Miriam on this occasion. Well, in 1 Cor. 14:34 Paul appealed to the law. He says, "as also saith the law," In the very passage he's been relying upon, Paul also referred back to the law, "As also saith the law." So he puts me in the same hole with the Apostle Paul, or puts the Apostle Paul in the same hold with me, whichever way he wants it.

And on Mark 7:14-23, where Jesus called the assembly, he said, "Porter said this is simultaneous teaching." Porter didn't say any such thing. I said that here is an example of taking one group from another group and teaching the group that is taken away. I didn't say a word about simultaneous teaching. Cecil wants all the details in one passage. I gave one passage for one detail; I gave another passage for another detail; but because we don't find all of them in one passage, why, Cecil won't have it. Yet he couldn't find the plan of salvation, every condition in the plan of salvation, in one passage to save his life, but he'll take it.

Then to the transfiguration scene in Mark 9. I showed

from this that the Lord took away a group, Peter, James, and John, up into the mountain, that God taught them, and that when they came down from the mountain the next day, Jesus Christ was teaching them. When they approached the disciples left behind, they found a religious discussion going on in that group — and there was the parallel of simultaneous teaching. What did Cecil say about it? Oh, he said, "The disciples went to sleep; that's like the Sunday School class." The disciples were not the teachers on that occasion, Cecil. God was the teacher, and he was very much awake. They were the ones who were needing to be taught, and in the second place, he said, "Peter proposed three tabernacles, and he knew not what he said — that that's just like the Sunday School class." But again I remind him that Peter was not the teacher upon that occasion. Peter was the one to be taught — he wasn't the teacher. And in the third place, he said "These teachers back there in the other group were without faith — they failed to heal that person, they failed to cast out the demons; so they were without faith." He said, "That's just like your Sunday School teachers — they were without faith." Well, the faith that they were without, Cecil, was *miraculous faith*, and *you don't have an "once" of it.* You don't even have an "ounce" of miraculous faith that you said they were without — not an "once" of it. You can't perform *any kind of miracle.* So that just cuts you out completely. And besides, remember this; that Jesus Christ was one of the teachers teaching one group. Yes, he was — he was one of them. And then again he said that "was a Holiness healing service that backfired." In other words, Cecil compared the disciples with the Lord Jesus Christ with a bunch of fanatical Holinists. The apostles of Jesus Christ — he's compared them here, and paralleled them, with a bunch of Holiness fanatics. That's the idea, for he says, "like a Holiness meeting that backfired," a "Holiness healing service," or something of that kind, "that backfired." Well, we'll pass on from that.

Now, then, he tried to draw his parallel on instruments and classes. I showed the instrument is not parallel with the classes. He comes back and says it is, that the singing excludes the instrument and teaching excludes the class. Well, on the same basis then, teaching excludes the radio. The fact is, if you use the class, you *do nothing but teach;* if you use the radio, you *do nothing but teach;* but when you play on an instrument, you're *doing something besides sing.* The cases still are not parallel. He said there are two additions — "Go, *play on the instrument* and sing." That's one, he said. "Go, divide into classes and teach," That's another addition. All right, as I gave you last night — "Go, *get you a radio microphone* and preach." So if we have two additions, we have three additions right there. The fact is, if you get the microphone, you do nothing but teach; if you get the class, you do nothing but teach, but when 'you get the instrument, you're doing something besides sing.

And he said the brother had no knowledge of the Montevallo church. Said the brother had no knowledge of the Montevallo church. Well, the brother that told me about that was one who had part in the work up there, Cecil. Again you didn't know what you were talking about.

Then there were three women that "fell out of the plane". I didn't say they fell out of the plane. But he wants to know if they could baptize and ordain elders. I asked him if they could worship God. Now, Cecil, God has not commanded those women to baptize and ordain elders, but he has commanded them to worship. So I want to Know *if they can worship,* if *they can do what God commanded them to do.* That's the thing that you skipped; that's the thing you dodge; that's the thing you side-stepped.

Then you said the Missionary Society is a means of teaching. No, the Missionary Society is not a means of teaching. The Missionary Society is an organization, a human organization, an addition to the church, that sends out men to preach *by the very same, that method, that Cecil uses.* Those preachers sent out by the Missionary Society go out and preach just like he preaches, upon the same method, the lecture method. And so the Missionary Society is not a means of teaching. It is merely an organization, such as *our Bible classes are not,* as I have contended all along during this time. I thank you, Ladies and Gentlemen.

Abercrombie's First Speech
Fourth Night — December 7, 1951 — (Negative)

Fellow Moderators; Ladies and Gentlemen, Worthy Opponent:

I am indeed happy to stand before you tonight to deny the proposition which has just been read. Brother Porter is here trying to prove class teaching, organization of the Sunday School, that churches of Christ have all over the country; he is trying to prove that it is scriptural to organize such, that is, the church, to group and grade it according to human wisdom, and have a plurality of teachers, having men and women teaching simultaneously when the church assembles. Now, that's what we are here to discuss, and so just a few remarks about last night.

It is not right for my moderator or my opponent's moderator to get up and insinuate that either of the debaters have refused to answer a question or argument. Every person is to be the judge of this discussion — not just one. Brother Dennis was perfectly in his right to ask about such matters as my moderator last night. Somebody might have misunderstood that. Moderators are to keep good order; see that all fairness is displayed, besides keeping time.

Now Brother Porter's proposition calls for a plurality of teachers in classes when the church assembles, women teaching in some of these classes. Now then, why does he skip all of those examples of the New Testament church coming together to be taught the word of God, and go all the way back to Moses? "The law was given by Moses, but grace and truth came by Jesus Christ." If you could find a replica of it over there, it wouldn't serve as proof today. The Apostles didn't use it. The Holy Spirit didn't guide the apostles to do that, and wrote commandments against such. I would like to say that I have not lost interest in publishing the Taft debate on this one. We will be glad to help publish it, what we can. I have answered Porter's quibbling, suppositions, all through this debate. He ignores question after question that I have asked him throughout my speeches. And, incidentally, I haven't given him 14 or 15 questions to keep him off his proposition. I want him to thoroughly commit himself and not be engaged in quibbling, teachnicalities that have nothing whatsoever to do with the issue, and that's what he did to me when he gave me those questions. However, they were answered. How do the elders oversee the teachings of women Sunday School teachers or how would they oversee such if she preached over the radio? You say she can preach over the radio if men don't listen in. You can see that he has got something there that is unauthorized by the word of God. *Since 1 Cor. 14:31 is twisted to apply by Brother Porter to Sunday School teaching, how do you keep verse 35 from applying there?* That says, "It's a shame for a woman to speak in the church." *"It's a shame for a woman to speak in the church," and that applies where 1 Cor. 14:31 applies.* These are just a few samples. Where is the church of Christ in the Bible with the Sunday School organization? Where is one with women teachers such as his proposition calls for when the church assembles? He cannot find it and of all scriptures, my friends, he has used one that is against him, and the only reason he used this he's going to try to explain it away, and he knows that if he can't explain in it away, then his cause is lost anyway, and there is no use bringing up any examples. He would call the church coming together and being taught by men who speak one after the other to all present, a class. We are talking about his Sunday School organization, teaching, and women teachers in such, and a plurality of teachers, and things of that kind. He would call this assembly a class teaching and he knows it's no such thing.

Now then to a few things said last night. On his chart he had their classes justified. He justified classes by the great commission to teach. Just as sure as he can put his Sunday School society in on the command to teach; the Christian Church can put a missionary society in on the same command. Both of them are teaching institutions or organizations. They are in opposition to the Lord's church. They are not found in the word of God. They have nothing in common with the Lord's church, the church of the Bible. Neither of them are mentioned in connection with New Testament churches of Christ. They are modern. They are not of God. They were not authorized by the scriptures. They are condemned by the word of God. Now then, we can put missionary society in on the same ticket that he brings in his Sunday School.

In Acts 5:25 and Acts 2:6-7, I don't believe that he noticed Acts, the second chapter and verses 6 to 7. That shows that there was a coming together, and there was the *present tense*, and it shows that they were all together and there were twelve teachers. And his iron-clad interpretation and strait-jacket that he puts on Acts 5:25 that is; when you find a plural in the present tense, therefore, then *all of them must be talking at the same time*. Therefore turn to Acts, the second chapter, and verses 6 and 7. We find the church come together, no division into classes, and then we find the present tense and there we find a plurality of teachers and he has twelve men teaching at the same time to one assembly. He knew that it was against him, and he knew it destroyed his contention on Acts 5:25. And on Acts 4:1 to 2, we find, "As they spake the chief priests and scribes and the Pharisees came upon them." I showed from the third chapter that Peter alone was doing the preaching, and that John concurred with his remarks. He expressed the sentiment of John. Whatever Peter said John believed it, and then we find in the fourth chapter "As they spake", using the plural. Though it is in the past it doesn't alter the case whatsoever. "As they spake", or "As they were speaking", they came upon them and there we see the plural used. According to his interpretation of Acts 5:25 we have Peter and John both talking at the same time to that one audience that gathered in Solomon's porch. They were not divided into classes. So he's ruined on that entirely. I don't claim to be such a smart man, don't know much, and don't have to know much to meet these things.

University of Georgia, Department of English, Athens, Ga., Feb. 18, 1943, wrote a letter to the head of the English Dept. What did it say? "My dear Mr. Abercrombie: My feeling about the phrase "are standing" is that it does not at all necessarily imply that everybody was talking at once", and he is an English scholar out here at Athens, Georgia, University of Georgia, head of the English Department. "We (now listen to his illustration) say commonly the two men are talking, the committee is talking, and so on without at all meaning that there was a chorus". (But he gets a chorus there. Every time he used that, it was a chorus, but he's certainly out of tune.) "In America we tend to regard collective nouns to singular, but in England people tend to think them plural. An Englishman would say "The jury are talking." He would not mean that everybody on the jury was talking at the same time. The progressive present is a very common tense. I am talking, I am singing, he is reading — this means progressive action in th present time, but the *tense* of the verb is not the point of your question. What you're interested in is the number; that is, whether the plural form of the verb necessarily means that more than one person was teaching at a given moment. I don't think it does. We say that Tech's swimming team are winning all the contests without at all of courses suggesting that all the Tech swimmers are swimming at the same time." I showed this to him up at Taft. He looked at it, and said that —

(Porter: Let me see the letter.)

(Abercrombie: I'm not through with it.)

He looked at this and said, "Why he answered according to his feelings." "His feelings." The very idea! A scholar giving what he knows as a scholar. That's what he meant by it. He answered, "It's his feelings."

We now turn to Mark 9:14 which he introduced last night to prove his classified assembly of the church; and begin reading at verse 14. Now, let's notice this. "And when they came to the disciples they saw a great crowd about them, and scribes arguing with them, and immediately all the crowd when they saw him were greatly amazed and ran to him and greeted him." Now I want you to notice the pickle this has him in. *He doesn't believe in a plurality of teachers speaking to one group.* But now let's get this: he has found one group that; (he's already stated that, because that's his analysis), one class coming down the mountain and the other class at the bottom, or somewhere on down. All right, "And when they came to the disciples they saw a great multitude about them, and *scribes (plural)* arguing with them". When? *Right then.* "And immediately when the crowd saw him, all were greatly amazed." Here are scribes arguing with disciples. *"Disciples" is plural, and "scribes" is plural, and he says that's a class.* Can't you see that he is bound, tied hand and foot. He's got a plurality of teachers argueing and teaching one group at the same time. He said, "I won't have that." No wonder he didn't mention that in his speech tonight. If he did I didn't notice it.

All right, we turn now to Luke 18:31 and 33. Here is another one of his proof tests for simultaneous classes, teaching when the church assembles. Now, the church wasn't established when this took place. It didn't occur until the day of Pentecost, but now he is using this to prove that you can do it when the church assembles. "Then he took unto him the twelve and said unto them, Behold we go to Jerusalem, and all things that are written by the prophet concerning the son of man shall be accomplished." "Behold we go to Jerusalem." Jesus had been teaching some people and then he went aside and took the disciples himself and started out up the road to Jerusalem. He said, "Now, there is proof for simultaneous class teaching." Isn't that ridiculous? A man of his ability to present a thing like that! When Jesus was teaching with all of them together including the disciples, well there was one audience, and we find that after he ceased teaching the mass or multitude, he took his disciples with him and went down the road, one teaching one group. He quit teaching, all — started on the road to Jerusalem. Where, oh where, is his simultaneous teaching? It's not there. He will have to do better than that. Where, oh where, is the women teaching in classes of that kind? Talk about answering questions! I've answered his until it's simply routine, but he ignores mine. How do you classify? How do you classify? If this thing was so important, and important enough to divide the Church of Christ all over the world it seems to me that he would be able to turn to the *chapter and verse* and find the scripture how to classify. And I *want to know how the elders oversee the women teaching in the classes since they cannot go in there and hear what she says.*

I've insisted that he has a new order of evangelists, women evangelist, for women only who are immune from the scrutiny of God's overseers of the church. No wonder so many "isms" are coming in through the Sunday School!

Mark 10:32 — "And they were on the road going up to Jerusalem and was walking ahead of them, and they amazed and those who followed were amazed and he took the twelve again" and began to tell them what was to happen to him. Verse 33 says, "Behold we are going up to Jerusalem", etc. No simultaneous teaching here; only one teacher and one group — talking at a time — no women teachers. Where is she, Brother Porter? Give us a New Testament church showing her.

Now then we wish to notice some other things pertinent to the occasion and that is a little more about this transfiguration. We find up there Peter, James, John, and Jesus. They went up there to pray, the scripture says. A miracle took place and this man took a position that since there was no miraculous gift today in church assemblies, (at Taft), therefore he threw it out. But he retreated from that when we showed him that tongues, miraculous gift, was in

Acts 5:25, to make a Sunday School out of that at Taft, Tenn. So if that would stand, my friends, he throws it out by the miracle on the top of the mountain, and a miracle performed at the bottom, *and so he hasn't a thing to stand upon.* Talking about the teachers up there, said God was a teacher. I thought that — Isn't Christ a teacher? There was Moses and Elias — they were teachers. Why yes, and they were talking about the Lord's decease in Jerusalem, the scriptures say, There we have four teachers — God, Christ, Moses, and Elias. Four teachers for one class on top of the mountain. Four teachers! I guess they were all talking at once! No instruction for the multitude to be taught while he was up in the mountain. They came down from the mountain the next day. He found a mixed multitude of confusion. Why? The disciples tried to cast out a devil, and evil spirit, and failed and they couldn't understand why. They lacked faith. Jesus said, "Because ye have a lack of faith." That's why I said it looked like a Holiness "supposed" healing service today, because they failed to heal. That was what the argument was about. *No one could doubt that it was public, yet Brother* Porter has now used something that is public to fit his simultaneous class teaching, which he says is private. Consistency!

Now then we have something else we would like to notice. Brother Porter has asked in my affirmative: time and again to bring in other things and debate it. I tried to get him to stay with the proposition and he would not do it and he just insisted to talk about other things. "Cecil is afraid for you to know his practice but Porter doesn't care whether you know his practice. He wants you to know it." That's what his arrogancy has displayed in this debate.

Look at this, brethren. The women in Sunday School classes can't be supervised because the men can't go in there. And look at this "Little Jewel, Gospel Advocate." It says, "You rememeber the good show he took us all to because Dick did not go on to the bad one." Go to picture shows, "Do you remember," Jim asked seriously, "that Dick's Dad would not let him go to the picture shows," and so on. Just take him to the good picture show!? Now pick out you show. *Here is another one teaching the Sunday School pupils to go to the picture show.* "When Alice in Wonderland comes we will go to the picture show." Just pick out you shows. Now I suppose the Church of Christ is going to have to do like the Catholics, set up a board of censorship and let all the elders and the deacons and the preacher see them to pass it on to the congregation and tell them which shows Hollywood is turning out that is fit to look at. That's something that is coming in through the Sunday School.

Here is some more — "Christmas, Birthday of Jesus Christ." Here is your *"record and rewards"*; there is you *Christmas tree.* (Literature and pictures exhibited by Brother Abercrombie.) Nothing in the word of God about such.

Here's the University Church of Christ directory and George Henry Peter Showalter is the preacher there and he has a Sunday School superintendent. Not just advertising books for superintendents in his catalogue, but he's got one in his church and Brother A. B. Cox was superintendent. 1936 — there it is.

Here we have Robert Raikes started the Sunday School. Church of Christ put this out. (Sunday School certificate exhibited.) There is a picture of his meeting house, all of that.

Here J. C. Roady said, "Just give us a little Sunday School to start with." That's how it came in.

My friends, here is Brother Porter's book called, "Ask you Preacher". He says, "Insist that the preacher gives a passage in the New Testament — where the church ever used musical instruments". Oh, yes, insist. I've insisted that he give the passage and show the church that used the classes, but it can't be found. We have not time to go into these things like we would like to. Just one other thing here and we shall notice these things as we come to them. Here we find from John Odowd (He, Porter, has been reading from my brethren's papers), "Brethren, let us have a house cleaning this season of the year and cast out of the presence of the Lord all traditions and organizations within the body of Christ, namely a sectarian oiled and groomed modern Sunday School patterned after the infidel institutions of denominationalism. Do not misunderstand me. I am not opposed to systematic Bible studying in classes, but the digression some brethren have gone to in Dallas." There you have it in sound words 1935.

Now then, let's notice this thing. Let's look at this thing up here on the chart. Let use see what he has in it. The apostle Paul says, "Let the woman learn in silence." He says that this is parallel to this. All right, in Acts 4:18 I'll show you that it is not a direct and absolute parallel in Acts 4:18. There is no comma before the nor, showing no break in the thought. Furthermore "nor" in this passage of scripture is from a different Greek connective than the one in 1 Tim. 2:12. All right, we'll laugh some more. In order to uphold their women teachers Porter contends that the only restriction here is that women teachers should not teach men; that is "over the men". So they must wrest this passage to read like this, "Let the woman teach with all subjection but I suffer not — (No, just strike out the "but"), "I suffer" (strike out the not) "I suffer a woman to teach" (strike out the comma before the nor — strike out the nor). Now he says "I suffer a woman to teach under the man but not to usurp authority over the man", (strike out the comma there — put a period and knock out entirely "but to be in silence".) Now then we have Porter's new version: "Let the woman teach with all subjection, I suffer a woman to teach under the man but not to usurp authority over him", and ignore "but to be in silence."

(Abercrombie asks for a piece of chalk.)

Let's fix this up a little. "But to be in silence". Now, that means she can teach just so she doesn't teach men, but she must do it in silence! She must use sign language! *Why didn't you put that up there?*

He said this is 1 Tim. 2:12. He knows that the eleventh verse goes with this and he deliberately left that off. He knew that it ruined his scratching up here on the board. I have here a letter from Vanderbilt University, Walter Clyde Curry, head of the English Dept., nationally known scholar: "In the King James Version of the Bible, 1 Tim. 2:12, the phrase "over the man" does not modify the verb teach in the preceding clause."

Furthermore I would like to notice also from the head of the Department of English, University of Georgia, this reading also: "Dear Mr. Abercrombie: In the verse that you refer to I should take the phrase "over the man" to modify the word "authority." This interpretation seems to make both gramatical and technical sense." I don't claim to know so much, but when some man gets up here and claims to know so much that he knows nothing, I will expose him to the limit. He just tried to display his knowledge up here. These said Porter, *do not* know what they are talking about.

Here we have Howard College in Birmingham: "Dear Mr. Abercrombie: Your letter of October 13, I have checked four different translations of the New Testament, 1 Tim. 2:12 in the King James Version reads: 'But I suffer not a woman to teach nor to usurp authority over the man.' In this sentence the phrase "over the man" gramatically modifies the noun authority. American Standard Version reads; 'But I permit not a woman to teach nor (something else) to have dominion over the man'. The phrase here, "over the man" modifies the noun dominion. Other translations such as Goodspeed, Weymouth, Knox give practically the same reading." P. P. Burns from Howard College.

Let's notice what's in that passage. Look what he left out. *"Let the woman learn in silence."* Why did he leave that out? "With all subjection". Where is the woman to learn in silence? Somewhere? It is in all assemblies of the saints. Paul said that "it is a shame to speak in the church". He wasn't talking about the home, for he said she can ask a man or a husband at home. Verse 34, this passage of scripture shows in connection with Paul that he talking about women teaching in church assemblies — "as in all assemblies or the churches of the saints. Verse 33 in 1 Cor. 14: "Let the woman learn in silence with all subjection, but (showing contrast) I suffer not a woman to teach." I do not suffer that. Where? Why, Paul said in the church, church assemblies, that's where. And he, knows that he's taken the position that the Sunday School is the church. That's what it is. Now the, "I suffer not a woman to teach nor to usurp authority over a man." I do not allow this. Now other scriptures teach that same thing. She cannot usurp authority over a man in a home or anywhere, but that doesn't apply to teach. She can teach a man where she can teach. "She can't teach a man" says Porter. Look at Acts 18:26. There is a case of a woman helping teach a man. Her teaching is private, personal, individual, and informal, away from church assemblies. She is not allowed to conduct church assemblies, to go forth preaching the gospel as an evangelist, but that man has established a female order of evangelism — gone with the Holiness! To usurp authority over the man, I don't allow that. But here's what I do suffer — "to be in silence." Now, that is what that man has presented here tonight. I would like to offer a parallel passage of scripture or so in this same connection — almost the same construction.

Matt. 7:6 "Give not that which is holy unto dogs, neither" (cude — Gk.) that's the same nor connected in Acts 4:18 "cast ye your pearls before swine." Now give this verse the same construction that Porter and Nichols put on 1 Tim. 2:12 and here is what we get. "Give not that which is holy unto dogs before swine." So brethren, be sure there are no hogs around when you give that which is holy unto dogs! Paul said, "We behaved not ourselves disorderly among you, neither (nor) did we eat any man's bread for nought." 2 Tim. 3:6-7. Now connecting the expression "for nought" there back with Paul's first statment we hear him say, "We behaved not ourselves among you disorderly for nought." Does that sound like the apostle Paul? 1 Tim. 6:17 also, "Be not highminded, nor trust in uncertain riches." Now does that mean that they can be?, The same Sunday School twist on this as he did in 1 Tim. 2:12; would make Paul teach, "Be not highminded in uncertain riches", highmindedness is permissible provided it is not connected with uncertain riches. I readily admit, friends, that as Brother Porter stated that a prepositional phrase can modify, that as he said on Acts 4:18 and does there, but as I have shown from these scholars it does not apply in this case for sentences have difference of construction and that's true of this.

Now then we notice just a little more — 1 Peter 2:22, here's another almost parallel. It's as parallel, even more so than the one he offered with 1 Tim. 2:12, "Who did not sin, neither was guile found in his mouth." Does this mean merely that Christ merely did no sin in his mouth? Why certainly not. But that's the interpretation or construction that Brother Porter has placed upon these things, and he shall not pass. God has taught three things in that passage of scripture. Where a woman is allowed to teach, she can speak to a man, woman, or child. Where she is forbidden to teach *she can teach no one.* Paul says, "Let the woman learn in silence with all subjection, but I suffer not a woman to teach." One is another thing, here's something else, "nor usurp authority over a man, *but it be in silence." The very thing Porter left off of his chart.* Left this off up here. Peter said "Some do wrest the scriptures." My friends, you have seen a demonstration of it tonight in the person of Brother Porter. Wresting and twisting the scriptures and leaving off, in order to try to put over a false doctrine that a woman can teach in church assemblies just so she doesn't teach a man. And do you know they get authority to teach in Sunday School assemblies of the church? — a man tells them to do it. And so if the same man told her to get in the pulpit that would be all right, too, because she wouldn't usurp authority over them. That's the only reason she can teach there. They allow her to do that, and if they told here to get in a pulpit she could do it then. That is the doctrine and teaching of this brother tonight, and that's what he is trying to palm off on you. We're going to examine 1 Cor. 14 and go into that as we have time. We have shown that Paul says, "I suffer not a woman to teach." We also find that Paul says that "It's a shame for women to speak in the church." This brother has something that he can't find in the word of God. Even his own brethren admit that it was 1700 years after the church of Jesus Christ was established. This man has something that he cannot put his finger on in one passage in the Bible and show one New Testament church with it, not one example can be shown. Not one can he give. The Bible is as silent as a tomb about this thing which has divided the church. This thing has divided the church.

I thank you kindly for listening.

Porter's Second Affirmative Speech
Fourth Night — December 7, 1951

Brethren Moderators, Brother Abercrombie, Ladies and Gentlemen:

For a little bit I want to begin where Cecil left off, or about where he left off. Then I shall go back to the beginning and follow his trail. But since his chart is now hanging on the wall, or on the board over my chart, I'm going to dispose of that first and then have my chart brought back to the audience.

Here he gives (Abercrombie's chart) on his chart 1 Tim. 2:12, which is a quotation of the passage, "Let the woman learn in silence with all subjection, but I suffer not a woman to teach, nor to usurp authority over the man, but to be in silence." He wants to know where this silence is to be. Why, certainly that doesn't change the meaning of it in the least. She is to be in silence *at the very place where she cannot teach over the man,* and that doesn't change the situation in the very least. If she is before a group of men, and endeavoring to teach a group of men as a public preacher might this audience, there is the very place she is to be in silence, the very place where she is not allowed to teach nor usurp authority over the men. And so he's adding the word "silence" before and after the passage but it doesn't change the passage. *Not one iota.* It stands just as it was before.

But he wants to knock out the "but" and cross out the "nor" and have Porter read, "I suffer a woman to teach". Well, that's what Cecil says, too. "Let the woman learn in silence with all subjection," but we will strike out the "but". "I suffer" — we will strike out the "but". "I suffer" — we will strike out the "not" — "I suffer the woman to teach anywhere except in the assembly." And so he says, "I suffer a woman to teach." Sauce for the goose is sauce for the gander, you remember.

Now, then, can we have this down? (referring to chart)

Brother Dennis, moderator. "Yes, sir."

I want next to call to your attention (chart no. 3) to some of the parallels he gave. With these (pointing to charts on blackboard) I showed that they commanded them not to speak at all not teach in the name of Jesus." Paul said, "If suffer not a woman to teach, nor to usurp authority over the man." And, of course, he added this down here, "but to be in silence". But I have considered that on his chart. It doesn't change the meaning of this at all. It shows that she is to be in silence at the very place where she's not to teach nor usurp authority over the man. It doesn't mention being silent everywhere, because Cecil doesn't say that — he even admits that she can speak in a public assembly at the eleven o'clock worship when she sings in the presence of men. But she is not teaching over the man in a case of that kind.

Now, then, he gave us the passage from the sermon on the Mount. Matt. 7:6. Jesus said, "give not that which is holy unto dogs, neither cast ye your pearls before swine." He says, "Now, that's a parallel with the sentence that Porter has here." And according to that Jesus said, "Give me that which is holy unto dogs *before swine.*" Therefore, if you give that which is holy unto dogs look around and see whether there are some swine. Cecil, is that all you know about English construction? If it is, I am sorry for you. The statement, "Give not that which is holy unto dogs, neither cast ye your pearls before swine," is a *compound sentence* made up of *two independent clauses.* The first clause, "Give not that which is holy unto dogs". That's an independent clause, and then the second clause, "neither cast ye your pearls before swine", is another independent clause. One is independent of the other. It is a compound sentence, and "before swine" has no connection under the sun with the first clause. But that's not true with this (pointing to diagram of 1 Tim. 2:12). You don't have two independent clauses here, Cecil. You have a simple clause with a compound infinitive. You don't have a compound sentence at all. Your case is not parallel. Write to the University of Georgia, or some of those places, and see if you can get them to straighten you out on that.

Then another he gave — I want to notice it. In 1 Peter 2:22: "Who did no sin, neither was guile found in his mouth." And, according to Porter, this would mean, "Who did not sin in his mouth." Now, this would make "in his mouth" modify both of them. But again you have the very same situation. We have here *two independent clauses.* "Who did not sin" — "who" is the subject and "did", the verb, and "sin" is the object of the verb. "Neither" is the coordinate conjunction that connects the two independent clauses. "Was sin found in his mouth" — "sin", the subject, "was found", the verb, and "in his mouth",

—162—

has no connection beneath the stars to the first clause. They're both independent clauses. But that is not true (pointing to 1 Tim. 2:12) of this up here. We have here not a compound sentence, not two independent clauses in this, but we have simply a compound infinitive phrase, used as the objective complement in both of these. Neither of them is parallel with those sentences which he gave. You ought to make a date with a grammar, Cecil.

Now, then, back to the beginning. He said it is not right for Brother Porter's moderator to insinuate that the questions were not answered as he did last night. Brother Porter's moderator merely made the statement that both men should answer questions. He directed his attention to both men, and the very fact that somebody hollered indicates that somebody felt guilty. And so that's all there is to that, and we pass it.

Then, he wants to know, "Why skip all the examples in the New Testament and go back to Moses?" I went back to Moses, not for authority in the church, but I went back to Moses as a parallel. I showed that under Moses there was a commandment to *teach,* but in that commandment to teach, they have had this sort of arrangement where there were 79,064 teachers, at least, placed over the men there enumerated; and, consequently, it required simultaneous teaching. I didn't go back to Moses for authority. I went back there for a parallel. It showed that if "teach" under Moses could involve an arrangement of that kind, then why cannot "teach" in the New Testament involve such as our classes, which is a very simple affair compared to this?

He didn't ask Porter a lot of questions to get him of the issue. And the questions I asked Cecil didn't get him off the issue either. They were not asked to get him off the issue, but evidently they *kept him off.* He was afraid to get into them. He was afraid to answer them because he would get into some issues he didn't want to get into. But he said they were answered. Yes, you know how they were answered. I'll leave that up to you. You remember how they were answered.

So we pass on to more matters. He wants to know how in the world can the elders oversee the woman if they're not in her classes? And if they don't sit in her classes and on the radio and things of that kind, how can the elders oversee it? How in the world can a building contractor oversee the building if he is

—163—

not to watch every nail driven and every piece of lumber sawed in two? And how do the elders oversee where *they* preach? After all these years of preaching, how many elders do they have anyway to oversee their work down at Union City? Better stay off the elders. Yes, how can I eliminate 1 Cor. 14:35? "How is Porter going to keep verse 35 from excluding women teaching in their classes?" I'm going to keep it from excluding women from teaching in our classes exactly the same way that you keep it from excluding her from singing, Cecil, for you say that she can sing in this assembly where she is forbidden to speak. You say that she can sing and confess Christ in this assembly where it's a shame for women to speak. How are you going to let them sing? How are you going to keep that from excluding singing? How are you going to keep it from excluding her from singing, Cecil, how are you going to keep it from excluding confessing Christ? How are you going to do it? It's in the assembly. Let Cecil show you how he's going to keep it out. I have already shown you how. Let him show you how he is going to keep it out according to his position. He can't do it to save his life. I won't have a chance to reply, but I would like to see him try to show us how in his next speech.

He wants to know then, "Where you can find a church in the New Testament with his system." He wants all the details of it. Yes, sir, he still contends for the details; he wants all the details on our teaching. "Where can you find in the New Testament a church practicing his system; where the church comes together, then they divide the assembly, then they go into this room and that room, and then some of the women do some of the teaching?" He wants all the details. I asked him over and over, "Well, Cecil, can you find a church in the New Testament practicing the details of this debate?" Where can you find that Paul ever challenged Peter for a debate? (They challenge for debates.) And in the second place, where can you find where they ever signed propositions, Cecil? And where can you find in the New Testament that they spoke alternately for thirty minutes each? And where can you find that James and John served as moderators? *Find the details.* That is what you are demanding. Do a little producing if you are going to demand that for the other fellow's teaching. Then give some of it for yours. Where can you find it? In the New Testament? No, he can get all that out of the command to teach. He doesn't need any details when it applies to what he does. When the other fellow does something, he wants all the details in one passage. That's characteristic of them.

The word "teach", he says, will include the Missionary Society as much as it will the Sunday School." If the Sunday School is a human made organization as the Missionary Society is, I would say "Amen". But that it is true of Bible classes such as we have, I deny emphatically. *I deny it emphatically.* The Society, Missionary Society, is a separate organization from the church and doing something else because they are simply sending out men to preach and teach, and those men are following the same system of teaching that Cecil follows.

Back to Acts 5:25 — Acts 2:6-7, "The men are standing and teaching." He said, "He didn't notice Acts 2:6-7." Oh, yes, I did. "They came together — *present tense.*" I showed, time after time, that the men said, "How *hear we* every man in our own tongue in which we were born?" "How *hear we* every man in our own tongue in which we were born?" Not "how *heard* we them", but "how *hear* we them", present tense. And that indicates that those men of differnent languages were hearing men speak in their language. "How *hear we* every man?" If all of them had to be in one group, according to Cecil, and if 3,000 converted on that day represents even ten per cent of them, that would make 30,000 people gathered there. That would require, if you allowed 4 square feet for each person, three acres for them to even stand together. and yet he has the thing all arranged that way, you see. And, consequently, that's where he stands.

Let's see again, Acts 4:1-2, "As they spake", He again admits that this is right, this is past tense, all right. But Peter was speaking alone — he was speaking for the rest of them. He assumes the same thing in Acts 5 — that Peter was only a representative. One of them was a representative for the rest of them, and he spoke for the rest of them; and, therefore, *they* are *standing* and *speaking.* Well, I want to turn to Acts 5:25 and read a little more in that connection. Right along just following that we will have a little more to say about it in verse 40. "And to him they all agreed; and when they had called the apostles and beaten them" (that is, they beat one of them that was to represent the rest of them), and "they commanded that *they* should not speak in the name of Jesus, and let *them* go" (that is, one them *shouldn't* speak as representative of the rest of them). "And *they* departed from the presence of the council" (that is, one of them as a representative), "rejoicing that they were counted worthy to suffer" (that is, Peter did the suffering, the rest of them went home). All of this is in the same chapter and in the same connection.

Then the University of Georgia — he wrote to the University of Georgia to Mr. John D. Wade to find out if this referred to a group of men teaching at the same time, and Cecil said, "I gave this to Porter over at Taft, Tenn., and Porter said, that is just his feelings about it, that is just the way he felt about it." And since Cecil denied it then, he denies it now. Let me read it to you.

Mr. Cecil Abercrombie, Union City, Georgia. My dear Mr. Abercrombie: *My feeling* about he phrase 'are standing' *is* that is does not at all necessarily imply that everybody was talking at once." Cecil said Porter misrepresented him when he said it was that man's feelings. *That's what the man said himself.* I didn't say it, this professor of the English Dept. at the University of Georgia said, "That's *me feeling* about it. That's the way I feel about it. That's my feeling. (Holds letter down for Abercrombie to see) That's what he said, didn't he, Cecil? Huh? Cecil said he didn't. Yes sir, this professor said it was his feelings. I didn't say it. The man himself said it. *"My feeling."* That isn't all we find in this either. Down toward the latter part of it we read again; "We say that Tech's swimming team are winning all the contests, without, of course, suggesting that all of Tech's swimmers were swimming at the same time." Therefore, it proves in Acts 5:25 that they were not all teaching at the same time. Well, let's see if it's a parallel. Let's try another case with that and see. I go to Professor John D. Wade, and I say to him, "Professor Wade, where is your Tech team?" And Mr. Wade says, "My Tech team is in the swimming pool winning a contest." That's the parallel with Acts 5:25. The man said, *"They are standing in the temple."* All right, let Mr. Wade say that *"they are in the swimming pool* winning the contest," and you have the parallel. But you don't have the parallel in the one that this man gave. Thank you, Cecil. You had better write again and have him fix that error.

Also he brought some others along that line. The University of Chicago, and some others, all claiming — well, that was on the other passage. I'll wait till I get to it. It's further down in my notes, I believe.

We come to the transfiguration scene. They came down from the mountain, and they found the scribes arguing with them, and Porter has a plurality of teachers at the same time. Well, there was a discussion going on, but that was religious instruction. There was discussion going on in the group that was left behind. And Jesus came down, teaching the group he took away. Jesus Christ was teaching that group at the same time there was discussion going on in the other. Suppose the others were wrong, Cecil. Just admit that the disciples and the multitude were wrong in what they did there. Just grant it for argument's sake. Was Jesus wrong when he was teaching while they were engaged in that discussion? When Jesus taught his group, as he approached that other group, *was Jesus doing wrong?* He was teaching at the same time the other men were teaching. And if it's wrong to teach one group while another man teaches another group, why, certainly it would be wrong for Jesus to teach one group while a dozen men taught another group, wouldn't it?

Luke 18:31 to 33 and Mark 10:32-33, "They weent up to Jerusalem." He said that Porter said, "Here is simultaneous teaching." *Porter said no such thing,* Cecil. Why don't you represent me like I said? Why do you come on here and just keep misrepresenting, misrepresenting, misrepresenting, saying things that you know that I did not say? Why do that? Why not come up here and deal with these matters honestly? I stated from the very outset that we have here *things that are parallel in one point and not parallel in every point.* And you admitted that that can be done. You admitted it last night. You said that was true. I gave Luke 18 and Mark 10, not to prove *simultaneous teaching,* but as a parallel of *taking one group from another group and teaching the group that was taken away.* I didn't say "simultaneous". Simultaneous teaching was on the Mount of Transfiguration when they came down. I gave that as simultaneous teaching. I gave this one for an entirely different point—that Jesus took one group from another group and taught the group that was taken away.

Oh, he said, "That was before the chruch was established." Certainly so — but did Jesus do wrong when he did it? Would not it be just as wrong then for two men to speak at a time as it is now? Wasn't it just as wrong back under Moses for *two men to speak to the same assembly at the same time* as it is now? Would God be the author of confusion then

— the author of confusion back in Moses' day—but not the author of confusion now? Why certainly that principle holds true throughout the whole time, Cecil. You haven't bothered it in the least.

He wants to know, "Where were the women?" I didn't say that there were any women there. I didn't give that to prove anything about women teaching. I gave that as a parallel of taking one group away from another group. And you missed the point that I made. You made no reply to that. You talked about something else—much easier to do it that way.

He wants to know *how to classify it'* "chapter and verse, please." Well *how* do you *arrange your radio programs?* Chapter and verse, please.

I Cor. 14 He said I threw this out at Taft, Tenn., because of the miracles. No, I didn't. The only thing I said about the matter at Taft, Tenn., was that you don't have an assembly like that anywhere, and I still say that he doesn't. But I did not throw out the principle in I Cor. 14. Yet there are some things in I Cor. 14 that are not true in his assembly or mine or anybody's else, as far as that goes. I never threw out the principles in 1 Cor. 14. That was just his jumping at conclusions. That's all. Concerning the mount of transfiguration, he said there was God, Christ, Moses and Elias, all teaching one class. Well, you have God, Moses, Elias and Christ all teaching one assembly. So what is the difference? You admit that they were taught; you said they were; you said they were all teachers—Moses, God, Christ and Elias were all teachers. They just had one class. He thought that meant something against Porter. Well, do you deny that they were teachers? *Do you deny that they were teachers?* Do you deny that they were teachers, Cecil? If not, then according to you, *they were still teaching the one class.* So that doesn't help it any.

Oh, how he "tried to get Porter to stay with the issue". but "Porter was determined that he wouldn't stay with the issue." He wanted Cecil's practice to be shown, so "I will just show some of his practice." And he brought up the Little Jewel, published by the Gospel Advocate, about the little shows and the good shows and the bad shows. I don't know what't contained in that. I'm sure I never did teach a thing that he referred to there. I'm sure that my brethren here haven't been teaching that; I'm sure of that, yes I'm sure that my brethren here haven't been teaching that; and I'm not sure that's taught in Dallas. Since Cecil misrepresents me as he does, maybe he misrepresents that, as far as I am concerned. I haven't had time to read it over. I would have to read it over first before I would know anything about that.

(Abercrombie offers to let him read it.)

(Porter: I'm sure that I don't have time to read it in this speech. No.)

But I assure you this, that if that is teaching children to go to shows, then I am not endorsing it. I repudiate or endorse wholeheartedly, Cecil, and you won't do either when I bring cases up. You just sit as silent as a tomb. Bring up something of that kind, and I'll either endorse it, or I will repudiate it. I won't refuse to take a stand, I won't evade the thing like you have been doing all the time.

And he said Robert Raikes started the Sunday School. I've been waiting for him to say more about that. He just mentioned that Robert Raikes' picture was on a certificate. That's all he ever said about it. But now he says Robert Raikes started the Sunday School. I don't know what he means by that. Do you mean, Cecil, that Robert Raikes is the man that started class teaching? Is that what you mean? I wish I knew, because I won't have a chance to reply to your next speech. I don't want to misrepresent you. I just want to know what you mean by that. Do you mean classes or an organized Sunday School? Which do you mean? They have always insisted that Robert Raikes started the Sunday School, and they imply by that that Bible Classes were started by Robert Raikes in 1783, 1700 years too late and too modern to belong to the church, he said. That's always been the idea along that line. Robert Raikes was the originator, the author, of classes. Now, that just isn't true, Cecil. Robert Raikes started some kind of school, all right, but he is not the one that is the author of classes. We find classes a long time back before him. Besides, Cecil, I've referred to the New Testament where Jesus took one group away from another, and where he divided the assembly, and things of that kind. Besides all of this, we can go to history, and find in history, a long time before Robert Raikes, that there were classes conducted.

For example, in the Manual of Church History by H. D. Newman Vol. One, page 271, we have this statement: "Shortly after the middle of the second century a catechetical school was established for the instruction of the children of believers." And then in the same book, Vol. One, page 296 and 297, we have the statement, "In the Alexandrian school, the catechemums were divided into classes according to their advancement." And that was in the second century, 1500 years before Robert Raikes was ever heard of.

(Brother Dennis, Moderator: "Let us read that, please sir.")

(Porter: "I'm not through with it yet — I've got another.")

And, then, again we have this statement from; A Concise History of the Christian Church by Martin Ruter, on page 54, (and this concerns the third century), "In general, however, sufficient time was allowed for instructing the catechemums in the doctrines of religion, *who were arranged in different classes.*" And that was back in the second and third centuries. I have the books in my suitcase up at Brother Fincher's room which these are quoted.

(Brother Dennis: "Oh, you haven't got them here?")

(Porter: "I havent't got them here, but I have them there. If you dispute my word, I'll send somebody after them. Do you want to dispute them?)

(Brother Dennis: "No, haven't got time.")

(Porter: "All right. They are up there. Anybody can see them that wants to.")

He brought up, "Ask your preacher." Yes, if a man insists on musical instruments, ask your preacher. Well, "I'm insisting on classes." Well, Cecil, I am insisting on radio preaching, and your cups, your plurality of cups in the communion service. What's the difference? When men play on an instrument, they *are not singing*. That's not a means of singing. But when he uses classes, that's only a means of teaching, which the Lord said do. When you use the radio, that's a means of teaching, which the Lord said do. It is not parallel in the least.

Then he came to John O'Dowd and the tirade that John O'Dowd made against certain wickedness and so on. And certainly every sinful thing that John O'Dowd condemned I'll condemn, too. I'll either endorse or I'll repudiate.

And then we come to the diagram. (Chart no. 3) We had

some of that already but we said, concerning this diagram, we'd get back to it. "These," he said, (pointing to the board) cannot be the same because up here they commanded them not to speak at all nor teach in the name of Jesus." he admits that "the name of Jesus" can modify both of these, because there was no comma, before the "nor". But down here, (pointing to other diagram) "I suffer not a woman to teach, nor to usurp authority over the man", there is a comma, and ait makes it impossible for this phrase to modify. (pointing to "over the man") There is a comma there.

Well, he talks about *exposing* somebody. I hate to do this. In Matt. 10:9, when Jesus sent his disciples out under the limited commission, he said, "Provide neither gold, nor silver, nor brass in your purse." There is a comma after gold; there is a comma after silver; and you have two commas instead of one; and yet will you deny that "in your purse" modifies all of them? "Provide neither gold, nor silver, nor brass *in you purse.*" According to Cecil, that will just have to modify brass. You can have the gold and silver somewhere else because there are some commas there, you see. Couldn't get them *in your purse.* There are some commas in your way. In order to get that *in the purse,* you are going to have to remove the commas. The commas block the thing, and you can't get it in there. My, my, Cecil! What next will a man do who is wresting the scriptures as you are?

And Acts 8:21. He said another thing about it is that *there are two different Greek words.* This word (pointing to first diagram) "nor" comes from a different Greek word from what it does down here. Yes, but they're both, according to Thayer's Lexicon, said to be negative disjunctive conjunctions. And we are going to notice something about this that we find regarding it in. Well, Cecil doesn't believe that she can't teach church assemblies. He has *already admitted* that *she can sing in church assemblies.* And singing is teaching. Therefore, *she can teach in church assemblies.* Cecil, this actually will not fit because you say that does not refer to church assemblies, for you admit that a woman can *teach in church assemblies* when she can sing. When she can confess Christ she can *speak in church assemblies.* And so you're wrong there, but if "teach" refers to church assemblies, so do the words, "usurp authority". They are right there together. "I suffer not a woman to teach, nor to usurp authority over the man". So if that means she cannot teach in church assemblies (she can teach anywhere else), that means she cannot *exercise authority over men in church assemblies,* but everywhere else she can. If it works in one case, it works the same way in the other.

And that gets down to the last thing you said. How does the woman manage to teach in the classes? He says she teaches there because man tells her to. That is the way she teaches without usurping authority over the man. The man tells her to. Therefore, if man tells here to preach the sermon at the eleven o'clock service, why, she can do that without usurping authority over the man. Well, many translations have it, "exercise dominion", or "have authority", or "have dominion over a man". And besides, she doesn't teach in the classes because man tell her to. God has already commanded her to teach, as I have already shown you from Titus 2;3 and 4. The Lord commanded her to teach, and Paul said she is not allowed to teach in such capacity that she would be exercising authority over the man. But if man told here to preach the gospel sermon to the congregation, it would not change at all what this says about it. This says she can't do that.

Now, that completes what he said, and I have about a minute or two, I believe. All right, I want to turn to this just a minute. (Chart no. 1) I showed you last night that we have some generic terms. The Lord Jesus Christ said "go". Go ye, therefore, and teach all nations." And that's a generic comand to go; and that command involves the various means of going. It may mean walk, swim, skate, or ride, and different ways of walking and different ways of skating and differnt ways of riding. It may be by riding in a car, riding in an airplane, riding on a train, riding in a boat, riding on a bicycle, or what not, but the bicycle and the train and the airplane are not mentioned in the book of God. Yet such can be done scripturally, because that's *a means of going.* If you ride, you do nothing but "go". If you walk, you do nothing but "go". Therefore, the means of going is involved in the command. The same thing with "baptize". It may be in a river, lake, pool, or baptistry, but in either case, you are simply doing what the Lord said, "baptize". And the same with "sing". You may use a song book; you may sing various voice parts; you may have a singing school; or an invitation song. All of those are involved in the commanded to "sing". And so with "teach". You may have a pulpit; you may have a printing press, a radio, classes;

but in all of them you are *doing nothing but "teach"*. So the command to teach involves those things. And the command to play, if there were one, would involve the various means of playing — the organ, the harp, the banjo, the violin; but "play" is *not a means of singing*. Play is not a means of singing as classes are a means of teaching. Absolutely not. Here is an arrangement for teaching. Play is not an arrangement for singing, and, therefore, they are not parallel; and Cecil Abercrombie has failed, miserably failed, to make any parallel along that line.

Now, I thank you very kindly for your patient hearing during this debate. I shall go into the presence of God at the last day with the realization that I must account for the things that I've said, and I am willing to meet him in that day upon the basis of the things I taught at this hour. May God bless you, and I thank you.

Abercrombie's Second Negative Speech
Fourth Night — Last Speech — Dec. 31, '51

I am indeed happy to stand before you once more in denial of the thing taught by my opponent in this discussion.

First I'd like to notice that concerning "Ask your Preacher". Brother Porter tells people, "Ask your preacher for the passage in the New Testament that tells instrumental music was used in the New Testament church. Find it." He wants the details. He can dish it out, but he sure can't take it. That's what he does with the Christian Church preacher. Brother, you tell me where it is. Tell me that New Testament church, give me the scripture for it. Then he says, "Does the church where you worship use any kind of mechanical instruments of music? If so, evidently your preacher sanctions their use. Do you know where Paul, Peter, James or John or any inspired man in that day ever used them or sanctioned their use in their worship? If you don't then surely your preacher does, if he teaches you to use them. Therefore go to him and ask him for the passage in the New Testament that says so", and he doesn't want details, does he? No, he doesn't want details. I have asked for details only in this discussion where God has given details. God has given details concerning teaching and that's the subject of this debate. He wants details and he wants chapter and he wants verse and he wants example for churches of Christ using mechanical instruments of music. But no, I can't ask him for such for his classified arrangement of teaching. No, that's all out of order for me to do that!

Then we have here this folder put out by the Church of Christ, 12th Ave. Church of Christ, G. S. Dunn, superintendent, Nashville, Tenn., and over here is what his brethren say about it, that "Robert Raikes, founder of Sunday School, 1780". Now, that's the kind they have. They have those patterns after Robert Raikes and we find over here a picture of his Sunday School, his first Sunday School. He's given credit by the authorities for starting the modern Sunday School movement.

Now then, he brought up and said they had classes and gave us some history about it, or before the days of the apostles or along that time. Oh, that's wonderful, we're glad to hear that. And now, since the apostles didn't use them *that's* all the more reason for our rejecting them. "They had them back there", he said, and they rejected them, didn't use it, and that's all the more reason for our rejecting such. If it had the mind, and will of God, and wisdom of God, to use such—if it met his approval and sanction, don't you know they would have used it while they had all the minds then, and capabilities and the capabilities of people, and they could have graded and grouped and classified them just like they group and grade people today! And so you couldn't set it aside from that stand-point. God had a better plan of edifying the church. He had a better one and that was for men to speak one by one that all may learn and all may be comforted from those men who taught. No division into the classes. Women were to learn in silence. Over here he said "class." Yes class—with him any group would be a class, whether it was simultaneously taught or not, whether it was divided up into a plurality of classes or not. We are here talking about this Sunday School organiza-tion of classes. We're talking about that, that's the subject of this discussion, and not about whether Jesus taught one group here or Jesus taught one group over there, and Brother Porter calling that a class. No, my friends, in all of the illustrations and the examples that he gave *he found my practice and what I'm contending for*—one teacher teaching at a time—and signally failed to find simuataneous teaching. He couldn't find it anywhere. If it could be found Brother Porter would certain-ly have brought it out. This man has perverted and twisted the precious word of God and his version reads like this: "Let the woman teach with all subjection, I suffer a woman to teach under the man but not to usurp authority over the man." That interpretation, my friends, will not keep her from teaching men. It certainly will not, if the man give her authority, telling her to do that. That won't keep women from teaching men. He's gone in with the Holiness and others who have a female ministry. That interpretation there will not, and you can see that. Let's read it again. "Let the woman teach with all subjec-tion." I'm not misrepresenting the man. "Let her teach with all subjection—I suffer a woman to teach under the man but not to usurp authority over the man." Now that's what he's taught here. And so if he would just quit protesting and give a woman the right to teach, just tell her to do it, she could go ahead and do it. His interpretation, therefore has released women to preach everywhere, and there's no escape from it.

Furthermore, he perverted the precious word of God in this — I want to turn to this once more. First we'll notice this: "Speaking Forbidden in Church." 1 Cor. 14:34-35. All right, let us turn to 1 Cor. 14. Here the apostle Paul is outlining the good order of teaching to prevail in all assemblies of the saints. Now let us read, beginning at verse 27, "If any man speak in an unknown tongue let it be by two or at the most by three and that by course, and let one interpret." Of course, it would be all right for them to speak in tongues without an interpreter in classes. But —

(Porter "Have you introduced that before? Have you ever introduced that argument before?) (This had been introduced the first night of the debate, and is found on my chart.)

Maybe not, we'll ignore that. All right. Let's get to the next one. I don't intend to violate any rules. "If anything be revealed to another that sitteth by let the first hold his peace." We have used this I know. "Let the prophets speak two or three and let the others judge." We've used that. "If anything be revealed and another sitteth by let the first hold his peace, for ye may all prophesy one by one." Now I want you to notice, he's speaking to the men — to the prophets — prophesy or teach one by one. Now he's regulating good order and teaching them how to do away with confusion, and showing them how to edify in the church when it assembles. All right. Let us notice it — "Speak (or prophesy) one by one that all may learn and all may be comforted." Now we've made this argument from the beginning and it is not new matter. Notice — men speaking in these assemblies one by one or by course — one after the other. And what is the result? "All learn and all are comforted." How? By hearing all of those teachers speak consecutively or by course, one after the other. Brother Porter says that's ours — we practice that. That applies to our clases. he does not practice it in his classes. He violated the teaching there. What is the comparison? You need only look at his practice and then look at what Paul said and you'll see the difference where he's twisting the word of God. He sets up a staff of teachers, a plurality of them including women teachers all teaching at the same time — to that given assembly of the church in various groups or classes, grouped and graded according to *his* wisdom.

When the apostle Paul said "Speak one by one, that all may learn and all may be comforted", and the spirit of the prohets are subject to the prophets, for God is not the author of confusion but of peace as in all churches of the saints", my brother here, and those with him, are setting aside God's divine plan of teaching, and edifying the church, and God's plan for doing away with confusion, by adding classifying, grouping and grading according to human wisdom. They are adding to the word of God. They are setting aside what God says. I want you to notice that verse 33 says that—"For God is not the author of confusion but of peace as in all churches of the saints." "All churches of the saints"—churches there is used in the sense of assemblies as we have before stated, and he hasn't denied it. It means all assemblies of the saints convened to teach the word of God. This order should prevail and therefore, since he claims immunity or something of the sort from doing just as this says and can organize classes and have them all taught—all the teachers talk at the same time—he has set aside God's wisdom and substituted the wisdom of man. Oh, when a man will do that it is a serious thing. "Let your women keep silent in the churches—in the assemblies—for it is not permitted unto them to speak." It is not allowed of women to talk or to ask questions or to speak in the manner and sense in which Paul was talking about here, in the very thing that we have argued throughout this debate. He was not talking about singing. He was not talking about confessing Christ before an audience. He was talking about women teaching and addressing the assemblies of the church. That's what he is talking about. Brother Porter agrees to that same thing, and his practice proves it. He, at eleven o'clock on Lord's Day, he says, "Sister, you cannot teach". The scriptures say "It is a shame for a woman to speak in the church", but I want every one of you sisters to sing." He makes the distinction himself and we have both agreed upon that throughout this discussion and I am glad that we can agree upon that. Paul was talking about women addressing assemblies of the church. Now then, let us read on. Here he says, "For it is not permitted unto them to speak, but they are commanded to be under obedience as also saith he law." This goes back to Genesis, and no doubt it referred to the law as a woman is to be in subjection unto man. That's the principle that God set up there for all time—that woman should be in subjection to man, and therefore we read the next verse. "For if they will learn anything," that is, if they would investigate God's word or learn more than that which they have heard in those assemblies, "let them ask their husbands at home." These wives of the prophets were not allowed to talk in those church assemblies. Those women should have been the wisest and smartest women in the church, being the wives of the prophets, inspired men, but even these women were not allowed to teach in these church assemblies. Why? What was the underlying reason? "For it is a shame for women to speak in the church." That's the reason. That's why Paul gave this law. "It is a shame for women to speak in the church." What came the word of God out from you, or came it unto you only? If any man think himself to be a prophet or spiritual let him acknowledge that the things that I write unto you are the commandments of the Lord." Brother Porter has admitted during this discussion that those men *must* speak as Paul has commanded. But he said, oh yes, that *just applies at one place.* We find in this teaching that it keeps them, when they assemble, it keeps them together so that all can hear, all those teachers. They must remain in that one place to hear all of those teachers speaking only one by one. If they weren't in one place how could they hear all of those teachers? Read and study verse 31. How could they hear them all? That shows the necessity of remaining together and therefore my proposition has been sustained and his has been utterly rebuted. Furthermore, he has put women in church assemblies and there they teach. "It is a shame" in the sight of God. Paul said these things are the commandments of the Lord. It is high time that men laid aside this high-handed way of mishandling and perverting and wresting the word of God and would acknowledge that what Paul wrote applied to all assemblies of the church to teach the word of God as he says here. "As in all churches of the saints." I have made that argument time and again, but I am re-emphasizing it for our benefit tonight since this is the last night of this discussion. I want you to have something tangible in your heart. I want you to know where you can go and read and find out what God teaches and not be befuddled by all the things that he has thrown in that are irrelevant and does not pertain to this proposition whatsoever and this practice. I want you to read and search the scriptures and see what God's word teaches.

Now, then, Paul said, "But if any be ignorant, let him be ignorant. Wherefore brethren, covet to prophesy and forbid not to speak with tongues. Let all things be done decently and in order." That is the grand and sublime underlying principle throughout that chapter. "Let all things be done decently and in order," and he has set forth the order that meets the approval of God's order and what God thinks is decent and in order when he told the men to speak *one by one* that *all would learn and be comforted and the women would learn there in silence.* That is giving an exposition of statements concerning the teaching of 1 Cor. 14:35. And the construction that my brother places upon 1 Tim. 2:12, will not keep women from teaching men. I want you to remember that. The only thing, that keeps women from teaching men according to his construction of that passage of scripture is because he will not let her do it. That is what he has taught.

Now then, let us notice some of the notes which I have taken. We turn to 1 Tim. 2:11-12, "Let the woman learn in silence." That shows that where teaching is being done, it's somewhere woman must learn there in silence. She is forbidden to teach somewhere — where she is learning. Now then, the apostle Paul has shown us that all are to learn from the men who taught one by one and be comforted. There we find he says "It's a shame for a woman to speak in the church." So therefore the woman is to learn in silence in the assemblies of the saints. That is the application of the apostle Paul, for we know that she is not silenced universally for she couldn't even teach or speak to her husband or children at home.

In Acts 18:26, we find there a woman helping teach a man. But this man (Brother Porter) has something that is unknown to the word of God. There are two categories in which women can teach. That is, they cannot teach in assemblies of the church — they can teach privately, individually, and in a personal way and in the sphere of the home, but she cannot convene assemblies of the church. In private and in an informal way a woman in her home may speak to a man and teach him something he doesn't know, and her children and women, and such like. But, we find that this brother parallels that with his class system and tried to justify women teaching from Titus 2:3-4 tonight. If that is a parallel then he's going to have to let the women teach the men in the classes because he has already admitted that women can teach men under such conditions and circumstances. Therefore since he will not allow such in the Sunday School the condition and circumstance there is not in harmony with that found in Titus 2:3-4. So then he has a new order that is unknown to the precious word of God.

Now let us read on: "With all subjection." "But I suffer not a woman to teach," as we have explained that — that's one thing that Paul does not suffer. And where is it that he does not suffer that? Paul said, "In assemblies of the saints." He does not allow that. Three things we have Paul saying here. "I suffer not a woman to teach" — one thing. "Nor, (something else) to usurp authority over the man." What else, Paul? *"But to be in silence."* I asked him, "Did it mean she could teach if she used sign language, for she had to be in silence?" You can see how illogical his chart was. He left off this entirely because it ruins his chart. This shows that she must be silent. And where is that silence? In assemblies of the saints. Paul says, "It is a shame for women to speak in the church." I want you to understand that *where a woman is forbidden to teach a man she can teach no one.* Paul is teaching that right there. Where she can speak or teach, she can teach a man. I have given repeatedly Acts 18:26. Why didn't he notice that?

We turn to 2 Peter. We will not use that, being new matter.

Titus 2:1 to 3, here we have (he used this — says that applied to his classes). In his debate at Quincy he said he didn't confine that to classes. No, he doesn't confine that teaching to classes. He knows that that has been done from time immemorial by God-fearing women in their home and private and in informal converstaion and in their homes. Yes so he has given that up. "House to house", women could go from house to house in a personal private and individual way, but she is not allowed to conduct or convene church assemblies or be an evangelist. But this man has established a female order of evangelists that allows her to preach only to women, but his interpretation of 1 Tim. 2:11 will not keep her from teaching men. I'm making that as an argument and I want to study it. The only reason he will not let her teach men is because she might usurp authority over him. And then he, man, tells here to teach in the Sunday School, and therefore, there she doesn't usurp authority because man tells her here to do that; and therefore if a man has a right to tell here to do that he could tell her to preach in the pulpit. You can see that his interpretation there sets in order a female ministry at large, irrespective of sex.

Matt. 18:20 — Here we find where two or three are gathered together, modified by the phrase "in the name of the

Lord." I've argued and showed that the Lord did not set up all-women churches of Christ. It is unknown to the word of God just like his Sunday School is unknown to the word of God. Women can teach men where she can teach — that same woman away from church assemblies in a private, personal, individual capacity. She is not to convene assemblies. Woman can teach children. Yes, but where do you find a New Testament church of Christ come together and dividing up into classes and some sister taking a group of little children out? He can't even find one thing that *remotely resembles his practice.* They didn't do that. They sat there and learned in silence. Women didn't assemble to *teach. They assembled to learn in silence,* "For it is a shame for a woman to speak (or teach) in the church." I have shown from the scholars that "over the man" modifies the word "Authority." Sentences have different construction and these scholars show beyond the shadow of a doubt that this modifies "authority." And he takes it and carries it on beyond that and makes it modify also teach and simply means that she could teach if she just didn't teach men. It is ungrammatical, it is unscriptural. These authorities have set that aside entirely.

What did he say about them? I gave you scholars to show that that was the case in the matter. I don't claim to know so much. I am sure that these scholars—they are recognized men with scholarly degrees teaching English in Universities, and he comes up here and tries to make you think that he is *superior in knowledge* to the professor of English at the University of Georgia, Howard College, and at several other colleges, at Vanderbilt. The thing is ridiculous.

Then he mentioned the invitation and someone confessing Christ. We have disposed of that. Paul doesn't have that under consideration whatsoever. Paul is not talking about that. But if that did apply it would also boomerang on him, for in that same assembly where he will take her confession he will not let her teach, but he'll take her confession, so it boomerangs on him. "Commanded to be under obedience." Elders tell women to teach in the Sunday School, therefore she is not usurping authority when the man tells her to do it. Therefore she can preach if elders would let her. That's Porter's logic. That's a logical deduction!

1 Cor. 14:31, he said I had misquoted that. Why sure, I have read it, read it time and time again right, and he has not

offset the teaching that I have shown to be contained in that verse of scripture. I read it again just a moment ago.

In Acts 4 we wish to notice this once more. Acts, the fourth chapter: "And as they spake unto the people the priest, the captain of the temple, and the Sadducees came upon them being grieved that they taught the people," using the plural form, and it showed, the context showed, that they were teaching when the people, the priest, the captain of the temple, the Sadducees came upon them. Yet the context further shows that Peter alone was doing the preaching. And so, John concurred with his remarks and we find the Bible saying, "They spake" when only Peter was doing the preaching. Yes, they only had one assembly. That's what confuses him. That's what gets them into trouble.

Furthermore in Acts, the second chapter we have here twelve men and one assembly. The multitude came together. What did he do with that? *Absolutely nothing.* He's higher than Haman. "And they were all amazed and marvelled, saying one to another, Behold are not all these which speak Galileans?" Verse 6 says, "The multitude came together" and then that multitude heard them speak. Yes, according to this interpretation and strictures upon Acts 5:25 when you find the present tense and a plurality of teachers, therefore it means all the teachers were talking at once, necessitating classes. But here he can't get any classes because it shows they were all together and his strictures on that have twelve men teaching one audience at the same time, and he won't have it. Oh, these things are certainly going before the judgment bar of God.

He said I arrayed Porter against his brethren. Porter insisted that I discuss foreign things and things that didn't have direct bearing upon the proposition. He wanted to bring that in and so I accommodated him, and then he squirmed under the lash in exhibiting to the world what his brethren are doing. Then he says, "I'll retract it, I'll fight that, I don't approve of it, I don't endorse that." I hope he succeeds in converting you brethren to stop this foolishness.

He said, that Cecil is learning. Mentioned the mistake on tense. I've gone over my notes very carefully concerning that debate and I find that I did make "one mistake" in that debate. It was on tense. And you know in my last discussion Brother Gus Nichols had been listening to that by wire recording and he said that Brother Porter made a mistake on that singing school argument, and he didn't use it in this debate, so he's learning too.

Then he brought up this assembly again. I am teaching one audience. The multitude of people. If people are all around this building and scattered across the street and they could hear my voice, I'd still be teaching according to the principle of 1 Cor. 14:31 and as Jesus taught when he sat in the ship taught the multitudes, so I haven't divided into a plurality of classes as Brother Porter has charged.

Then he said he didn't believe in one teacher teaching several groups. He turned right around and charged me with doing the same thing because somebody, he said, was in the basement. I didn't go down there. Might have been somebody standing out there behind the wall for all I know.

Old Testament simultaneous teaching shows "able men." Yes, and I showed that in order to get his parallel complete he ought to get Miriam in there, but he didn't want Miriam in there, 'cause Miriam upset the apple cart. No sir, Miriam just couldn't have a place in there. But if he's going to find a parallel in principle why doesn't he find that in the Old Testament? He said that his proposition was two-fold. One was simultaneous teaching and the other was women teaching some of those classes which are taught simultaneously. Therefore why didn't he go ahead and find the parallel concerning the women teaching some of those classes? I didn't just restrict that to the illustration you gave. You could have gone somewhere else in the Old Testament. As I have stated, if he could find his Sunday School just like he has it with the Gospel Advocate publishing the literature, it would be no proof today, my friends, to do that in churches of Christ. We are under the law of Christ and not under the law of Moses. No wonder he went to Moses' law because he couldn't find any illustration of his practice in the New Testament.

Why do not have time to go into all things as we would like. This debate is now before you. I want you to carefully and prayerfully consider what has been said. What I have said, I have said in all the earnestness of my soul. I am not trying to just be cranky or contrary or different from people. I love the Lord Jesus Christ and His precious gospel, and I want to see people walking in unison with God and His divine commandments. Oh, my friends, my prayer is out for everyone, that you might come and be obedient to the precious word of God. Follow his teaching, do not go contrary to it. Examine and weigh all the scriptures which have been offered in this debate and then you can come to a conclusion of who has the truth in this discussion. We are standing before God and we shouldn't follow courses just to be popular or anything of that nature, or follow multitudes or anything that is just modern, but we should follow that which pleases God in everything. We're going to have to meet before God all the deeds done in this body according to that which we have done, whether it be good or bad. I hold no ill will toward these brethren who differ with me. I love them. In all the earnestness of my soul I have pleaded with you to see the truth of the Lord Jesus Christ. I did not come here to engage in frivolity and things of that kind. I came here to teach you the precious Gospel of the Son of God, and tonight I have set forth from the scriptures those things that I am sure everyone could concede and will concede are the things that God would have us do, especially dealing with the two subjects which is so important, of teaching the word of God to the lost and dying. There is no plan under the heavens better than the plan which I have read to you tonight in the precious word of God, and so therefore in the face of God in high heaven let us be obedient, let us be submissive unto the will of God in all things. We thank you for you kind attention.

The End

www.ingramcontent.com/pod-product-compliance
Lightning Source LLC
Chambersburg PA
CBHW030714110426
42739CB00029B/228